The AMAZING DAD

D0572392

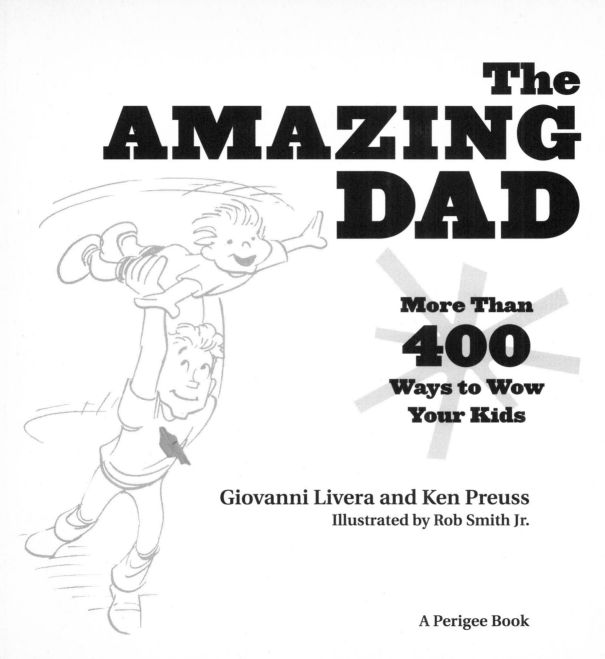

The AMAZING DAD

More Than 400 Ways to Wow Your Kids

Giovanni Livera and Ken Preuss

Illustrated by Rob Smith Jr.

A Perigee Book

Perigee Books
Published by The Berkley Publishing Group
A division of Penguin Putnam Inc.
375 Hudson Street
New York, New York 10014

First edition: May 2001

Published simultaneously in Canada.

The Penguin Putnam Inc. World Wide Web site address is
www.penguinputnam.com

Library of Congress Cataloging-in-Publication Data

Livera, Giovanni.
    The amazing dad : more than 400 ways to wow the kids / Giovanni Livera and Ken
  Preuss ; illustrated by Rob Smith, Jr.
        p.   cm.
    ISBN 0-399-52696-X
    1. Father and child—Miscellanea.   2. Amusements.   3. Creative activities and seat work.
  4. Games.   I. Preuss, Ken.   II. Title.

  HQ755.85 .L588 2001
  306.874'2—dc21

                                                                00-051673

Printed in the United States of America

10   9   8   7   6   5   4   3   2   1

Dedication

To my grandfathers, Dominick Livera and Earl Meyer, my uncle, William H. Dickinson, and my father, Giovanni Livera Sr. Thank you for playing the role of The Amazing Dad for my siblings and me.

With all of my love,
Giovanni

To my parents, Bernie and Donna, who created wonderful moments while raising three active boys. To my wife, Sherrell, The Amazing Mom who inspires me every day. To my son, Jaret, whose joyful imagination allows me to relive my childhood.

Love Always,
Ken

Although this book is a celebration of fathers and children, it is dedicated to others as well. It salutes moms, grandparents, aunts and uncles, older siblings, family friends, teachers, nurses, counselors, and anyone else who instills wonder and laughter into the lives of children.

Contents

PART I
The Amazing Dad as
The Acrobat of Anatomy

PART IV
The Amazing Dad as
The Chauffeur of Shenanigans

PART V
The Amazing Dad as
The Amazing Dadini

PART VI

The Amazing Dad as

The Greatest Showman on Earth

PART VII

The Amazing Dad as

The MVP (Most Valuable Pop)

PART VIII
The Amazing Dad as
The Maître d' of Mayhem

PART IX
The Amazing Dad as
Mr. Mystery

PART X
The Amazing Dad as
The Ultimate Friend

Introduction

You are a father. You are the most important man on the planet. You are the maker of moments . . . the creator of memories . . . the ultimate hero in the eyes of your child! It's a pretty good gig that's going to get better. You are about to become . . .

The Amazing Dad!

Don't get us wrong. You were destined for greatness long before you opened this book. Your kid has looked up to you for years (and not just because of your height).

You already possess a superpower. You have the ability to bring wonder and laughter into your child's world. It is a rare gift that should be treasured deeply. We're just here to help you develop it.

It's a fact of fatherhood: You work to provide for your kids. You work to protect them. You work to teach them right from wrong. And what do they remember? How you *play*.

The pages that follow are packed with magical moments that will captivate your child's imagination; foolproof bits of fun that have been passed down by fathers, grandfathers, and nutty uncles who only seem to come around when someone is serving a holiday dinner.

Many of the ideas will be new to you. A few may be variations on moments you have already mastered. Some may be childhood favorites that have been buried in your memory, waiting to be rediscovered and relived.

Reading this book will produce more fun than you can possibly imagine. It will provide you with powers beyond your wildest dreams. It will present you with secrets for sharing moments that will create lifelong memories for you and your kids.

It's in your hands. Turn the page! Transcend the ordinary! Transform yourself into The Amazing Dad!

Hints on Hiding This Book

The Rule

A superhero has to be sneaky. It's part of the persona. It maintains the mystique. As The Amazing Dad, you are required to follow suit (even though you don't have to wear one).

Your deception is simple: **Do not reveal the source of your superpowers!** Convince your kids that you were blessed with your astounding skills at birth. Never let them see you reading this book.

The Rationale

What would happen if Superman began changing his costume in front of the public? He would spoil the illusion. People would see that he was nothing more than a geeky guy with strange tastes in undergarments.

You don't want this to happen to you. (We're referring to the "spoil the illusion" part, though you should probably avoid the undergarment thing, too.)

The Ruse

Trust us on this one. To maintain your status as a superhero, you're going to have to hide this book. Read it when the kids aren't around, then stash it away so they never know it exists.

Stick it in the closet in a box marked "Tax Forms." Slip it in your dresser beneath a pile of socks. Set it on a shelf wrapped in a homemade book cover entitled, *The Joy of Spinach.*

The Relationship

When it comes to the kids, mums the word, but what's the word on Mom? Should you let your significant other in on the magnificent secret?

We say yes. Show her the book. She probably bought it for you anyway. (We had no problems believing Superman could fly, but we never bought the fact that Clark could keep secrets from the woman he loved.)

When you acquire an ally you become a dynamic duo. Your partner can read along and develop superpowers of her own. She can distract the kids so you can dash in and find ideas. She can even help you find the book when you've forgotten where you hid it.

The Reassurance

Hiding the book is an easy thing to do. It's a fun thing to do! It's the right thing to do! We gathered the information so you could get the glory. We want you to be the hero. Your *kids* want you to be the hero, too.

Keep reading! Keep learning! And, above all, keep quiet!

Before You Begin

Safety First

We want you to be The Amazing Dad! We want you to master as many moments as you can. We want you and your kids to have as much fun as humanly possible. We just don't want anyone to get hurt.

There are hundreds of great secrets in this book. There are exceptional ideas for children of every age. Look them all over, then learn the ones that are appropriate for your kids. Consider your child's age, strength, and maturity before trying something out. Consider *your* age, strength, and maturity, too!

If you have any doubts about your child being too young to appreciate an illusion or participate in an activity, simply save it for the future. You are going to be The Amazing Dad for a long, long time.

The Pronoun Predicament

We wrote this book for your enjoyment. We want these words to speak directly to you, as if we are old friends sharing secrets. The problem is we have no clue how to refer to your kids. You could have one son, one daughter, or any combination of both. We tried everything to create a solution.

Some attempts were too confusing: *Lift his or her hands over his or her head then tickle him or her under his or her elbow causing him or her to burst out laughing.*

Some were grammatically incorrect: *Make faces at your child until they smile.*

Others were too impersonal: *Take your kid and hug it.*

There was even an ill-conceived experiment with a gender-neutral name: *Have Pat bend Pat's arms and place Pat's hands on Pat's head.*

In the end, we opted to use one pronoun per item and alternate between them. We placed the pronouns randomly throughout the text with no attempt to assign gender roles. Any item featuring the word *she* is just as suitable for a *he* and vice versa.

If you see a pronoun that doesn't speak directly to you, do not skip the activity! Simply read the item, substitute the proper pronoun, and proceed. (You can even take a pen to the page if it helps. It's your book!)

The Dexterity Dilemma

Here's some handy advice concerning the words *left* and *right*. We alternated between them, too. If you are told to do something with your left hand, you can use your right hand and you won't go wrong. (As long as you remember to use your left hand when you're instructed to use your right.)

Did you get that right? Hope so. That's all we have left to say about it.

Ready . . . Set . . . Go!

The information you are about to read is astonishing, in quality as well as in quantity. The wealth of wondrous material is likely to leave you baffled as to where to begin. Here's our practical advice: Begin by practicing.

You are about to assume the role of The Amazing Dad. You are going to have a great time, but you are going to have to take it seriously. You must never attempt to unveil a superpower until you are certain you can perform it perfectly. (Running from the room in the middle of a trick to peek at a book that isn't supposed to exist is about as unheroic as it gets.)

So, show a little patience before you show off for the kids. Adapt the bits so they fit your personality. Rehearse the moves. Memorize the lines. Develop the timing. Do whatever it takes to become comfortable and confident.

When you are ready to perform, go for it. Present the material with all the pizzazz you possess. Have fun! Don't hold back! Give it your all! Commit to the performance and create some Amazing Dad moments that your children will cherish forever.

PART I

The Amazing Dad as

The Acrobat of Anatomy

1
Daddyland
Converting Yourself into an Amusement Park

Open the gates to a world of adventure and give your kid the ticket to an instant theme-park vacation. Create a series of sensational rides that provide twists, turns, and unexpected thrills. It's an out-of-your-body experience you'll both be sure to love.

Roller Coaster

Squat down so your kid can climb on your back. His hands should hold on to your shoulders and his legs should go under your armpits. Lock him in safely by pushing your elbows toward your sides and gripping his ankles with your hands.

Lean back and rise slowly as if going up an incline, then lean forward and move quickly as if plummeting down a hill. Run along an imaginary track filled with sharp turns, unexpected drops, and crazy spirals, then end up right back where you began.

Don't forget to add roller-coaster noises: the clicking of the track when rising up, the roar of the wheels when zooming down, and the release of the air brakes when coming to a stop. If you do your job right, your kid will provide the most important roller-coaster sound of all: the screams of laughter.

Antigravity Machine

Hold your child securely by the waist so she can bounce like an astronaut. Support her as she walks up the walls and across the ceiling.

DUH (Dad's Useful Hints): Make sure your space explorer wears the proper footwear. If her socks are clean when she begins her journey, your walls will be clean when she's through.

Super Slide

Sit on the edge of a chair with your legs inclined to the floor like a slide. Guide your child as she slides from your waist to the tips of your toes. Place a soft pillow at the bottom for a fun landing pad.

Flight Simulator

Lie on your back, bend your knees, and keep your feet flat on the floor. Have your child face you with his waist balanced on your kneecaps. Hold his wrists with your hands and extend his arms like the wings of a plane.

Tilt him up for takeoff. Raise and lower your knees to change his altitude. Lean left and right for trick maneuvers.

FLOOD!

Triple-Trouble Treetop Thrillride

EARTHQUAKE!

Extend your arms like the branches of a tree, and tell your child to climb your limbs. (You may wish to bend a knee as a foothold for your child.)

As soon as she begins, make the sound of rushing water and yell, "Flood!" Sway back and forth as if being struck by passing waters, making her climb playfully perilous. When she reaches a safe spot, stop swaying as if the water has stopped.

Stand calm for a moment, then begin shaking. Shout, "Earthquake!" and build the intensity of the tremors until she is holding on tightly (use your hands to support her when necessary). Hug her tight as the earthquake subsides.

While still in the hug, begin to spin slowly in place and scream, "Tornado!" Break into a running spin as if you have been uprooted and carried away. Fake a few near crashes, fall to your knees, and tumble safely to the ground. Kiss your child for surviving the ride and laughing in the face of danger.

TORNADO!

Wheeeee

Pony Ride

Strap a belt around your chest so your child can sit on your back and hold on. Drop to your hands and knees and take a leisurely stroll around the yard. Add a little horseplay by bucking your back legs, lifting your front legs, or stopping to graze before breaking into a gallop.

POP TEN LIST
The Daddy-Go-Round: Ten Ways to Spin Your Kid

1. Your hands holding his armpits.

2. Your hands holding both her wrists.

3. Your hands holding one of his feet and one of his wrists.

4. Her belly on your head. Your hands on her sides for support.

5. His belly on your shoulder with your arm wrapped around his back.

6. Her belly across your extended arms. Her body stretched as if flying.

7. His body above you. Your arms extended up like shooting a basketball.

8. Her body at your side. Your arm around her like carrying a football.

9. His body sitting on your shoulders in a revolving piggyback ride.

10. Her arms around you and your arms around her in a revolving hug.

Digit Deceptions

A Handful of Finger Fun

If you are looking for a great way to entertain your kid, you can always count on your fingers. Grab your kid's attention with some of these finger tips, and you'll be sure to earn two thumbs up.

Remove a Finger

Extend the left hand, folding the tip of the index finger back. Replace the folded tip with the bent right hand thumb. Cover the seam with the right index finger and pull hands apart.

DUH: (Dad's Useful Hints): If your thumb is too fat to pass as the tip of your index finger, fold the tip of the left thumb and remove it instead.

Add a Finger

Prove your child has eleven fingers with deceptively simple math. Have your child hold up both hands so you can take inventory. Count the fingers on one of her hands by going backward. "Ten, nine, eight, seven, six . . ." Quickly point to her other hand and say, ". . . plus five is eleven!"

Break a Finger

Hold your right hand flat with the palm up and the fingers spread. Grip the right ring finger with your left hand, squeezing as if trying to break it.

Bend the ring finger back. Secretly make a sound by snapping your left index and middle finger together. Since the snapping action is hidden beneath your right hand, it will sound as if you have broken the finger.

Find a Finger

WHAT YOU'LL NEED: Small cardboard box with removable lid • Cotton balls • Ketchup

Get a small cardboard box with a removable lid. (Mom's earring boxes work great. If she doesn't have an earring box, forget the finger gag and go buy her something!)

Cut a hole in the bottom of the box and slip a finger in. Surround the finger with cotton balls and pour on a little ketchup. Place the lid back on. Hold it with both hands so it's not obvious your finger is missing, then show your kids what you've found.

Fool a Finger

Ask your child to cross his wrists in front of him and intertwine his fingers. Next, have him bring his arms up so the intertwined fingers rest on his chest. Point to one of his fingers and ask him to move it.

Since his hands have switched sides, he will likely wiggle the wrong one, then giggle until he gets it right.

Pull a Finger

This book just wouldn't be complete without this fatherly classic. If you don't know it, we're not going to teach it to you. Ask another dad to explain it. It's a real gas.

Using Your Head
Fantastic Facial Follies

**Do something funny with your face and your kids will crack up.
It's probably a conditioned response dating back to early
games of "got your nose."
Want proof? Raise some hairs with these eye-popping gags
and watch them laugh their heads off.**

Proboscis Propeller

For a funny flight of fancy, turn a toothpick into an airplane propeller that actually spins on the tip of your nose.

Carefully break a round toothpick so there is a small crack in the center. Bend it back to its

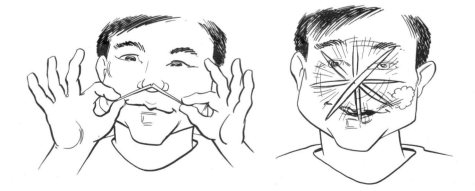

original position, closing the crack so it clips on to a small hair at the tip of your nose. Blow upward from the side of your mouth and the toothpick will spin.

DUH (Dad's Useful Hints): This is a *nose* hair, not a *nostril* hair. Think propeller, not ceiling fan!

Crackable Nose

Here's a snappy gag that allows you to fix your voice by breaking your nose.

Speak to your kid in a funny voice. Explain that your nose has snapped out of place and that you are going to snap it back. Bring the fingers of both hands against the sides of your nose as if squeezing it. Bring the sides of your hands together, covering your mouth. Pretend to break the nose by shifting the hands sharply to the left or right. Create a cracking sound by snapping a thumbnail against your top teeth.

Crack it a few times, trying out comical voices until you've returned your nose to the normal position.

Washable Eyes

Create an unexpected sight by trying to improve your vision. Remove and wash your eyes in full view of your child!

Reach your right hand to your right eye and make a pinching motion. Close the eye as you pinch so it looks like you have removed the eye from the socket. Bring the hand down quickly and pretend to pop the eye into your mouth like a grape. Repeat the same motions with the left eye.

When both "eyes" are in your mouth, swish them around like you are rinsing with mouthwash. Give shape to the eyes by pushing your tongue around the insides of your cheeks. Finish washing. Pretend to grab both eyes out of your mouth and pop them back into the sockets at the same time.

Open your eyelids slowly to reveal your eyes horribly crossed. Reach up, remove both eyes, cross your hands, and pop them back in the correct sockets.

Controllable Tongue

Press your nose with an index finger. Stick your tongue straight out as if the pressing released it.

Tug your right earlobe and move your tongue to the right. Tug your left earlobe and move your tongue to the left. Repeat a couple of times, then pull both lobes simultaneously to return the tongue to the center.

Tug the skin under your chin to slide your tongue back into your mouth.

Uncloggable Ear

WHAT YOU'LL NEED: One cotton swab • Cheese spread

Here's an unusual gag that allows you to remove something unexpected from your ear. It's one of the cheesiest tricks you can possibly pull.

Begin by dipping a cotton swab into some cheese spread. (Yes. You read that right. If this part sounds a little gross, you may want to move to a new trick.) Wait until your kid talks to you, then act as if you are having trouble hearing. Lift the cotton swab to your right ear, keeping the cheesy side hidden in your palm so only the clean side is in view.

Turn your right ear away from your child and make faces as you pretend to clean it. Secretly flip the cotton swab around, then turn back slowly. Present the cotton swab so your kid sees it at the same time you do and punctuate the gag with an incredulous, "Cheese!"

AMAZING DAD MOMENT
The Amazing Teeth of Great-uncle Harvey

I met Great-uncle Harvey when I was five. With a wink, he tugged his right ear and his top teeth dropped out. He yanked his left ear and his bottom teeth fell out. He pushed his nose and all his teeth popped in. He tugged both ears and all the teeth appeared.

My brother and I were delighted, astounded, and entertained. Then he wanted us to do it, too.

As we tried and failed, Great-uncle Harvey pointed out that obviously we were doing something wrong, "Why don't ya try pulling on your teeth while tugging on your ears and get 'em loosened up?" We couldn't figure out why he could do that and we couldn't.

It was a few years later that I learned about full-plate dentures and discovered Great-uncle Harvey's amazing secret.

4
Slap It Together
Five Funny Fives

The history of giving fives has seen its highs and lows. It's a touching greeting that seems to have lost some of its flair. You have to hand it to The Amazing Dad though, his fives are still a hit. Here's the skinny on five ways to give some skin.

The Body Quake

When your kid slaps you five, start shaking your right hand like it is wobbling from a spring on your wrist. Hold the hand out and ask her to grab it so it will stop shaking. Let her grip stop it, then start shaking your left hand the same way. From here on, just stay a step ahead of her.

If she lets go of your right hand to grab the left, start shaking the right one again. If she grabs both hands, start tapping a foot. If she steps on the foot to stop it, start tapping the other one.

Flap any extremity that becomes free until she is standing on both your feet and holding both your hands. Pause, until she thinks she has saved the day, then shake your head and flap your lips. Whether she leans her forehead up to stop your lips or simply lets go and laughs, reward her heroic efforts with a hug.

The Windmill

When your kid gives you five, let the force drive your hand down so your whole arm spins behind you and crashes on the top of your head. Look up to see what hit you, then back at your son to ask if he saw something bonk you on the head. Shrug off his response and ask him to give you five again. Repeat the move a couple of times, becoming more flustered in your attempts to figure out what is bopping you.

For a finale, announce that you will turn around fast so you can see what it is. When your son smacks your hand, turn your upper body to look behind you so the revolving hand crashes down flat on your face. Turn back with a silly smile to show you are okay, wince, and wobble away.

DUH (Dad's Useful Hint): Since your face is turned away, you can make the final crash look painful without causing any actual pain.

(One Hundred and Eighty) Five

Walk toward each other with your right hands raised above you in a high-five position. Swing and miss the high five, but let your arms continue their paths so they strike a low five as you pass.

SLAP!

Homemade Handjive

Write a silly rhyme and create your very own handjive routine. Here are some hints to help you get started:

Change Directions	Change Locations	Change Fingers
Five to the left.	Five on my elbow.	Give me three
Five to the right.	Five on my wrist.	Give me two.
Five to the middle	Five on my foot.	Four for me.
With all your might.	Five on my fist.	One for you.

Fast-Five Game

Have your child hold his hands faceup in front of him. Stand in front of him and place your hands faceup underneath his hands. Wiggle your fingers, then quickly flip one of your hands over, trying to give him five before he can pull away.

Giving a successful five earns you five points and a chance to try again. A swing and a miss, and you switch places. A player who pulls away before a five is attempted loses five points. The game ends when someone reaches twenty-five.

Make sure everyone refrains from getting slaphappy (hitting hard enough to hurt).

PART II

The Amazing Dad as

The Architect of Adventure

5
Fantastic Forts
Easy Instructions for Dynamic Designs

When your kid wants to have a campout, form a club, or simply hide away from the world, it's your duty as dad to provide a little space. No matter when and where the construction occurs, imagination is the most important tool.

Outdoor Forts for All Seasons

Winter
The Frozen Fortress

This creative castle is the perfect sanctuary for snowball combat. Form four solid walls of piled-high snow. Build the back wall over a board so you can tunnel an entrance underneath.

Top the walls with castle cutouts, or merlons, that you can hide behind and throw between. Line the inside of the walls with a shelf so you can stack and grab snowballs without having to bend to the ground. Build two and have the ultimate snowball battle.

Spring
Backyard Cabana

As nature comes into full bloom, take time out to create a shady spot that will let your kids kick back and observe their surroundings. Stretch a rope between two tall, stationary objects.

Drape a tarp over the top, then stake the ends into the ground. (If you use a couple of sheets, just connect them together with clothespins.)

Summer
Pool Palace

WHAT YOU'LL NEED: Four four-by-four posts • Two two-by-four posts • Two plastic pools • Nails • Sprinkler • Hammer • Post Digger

Help your kids beat the heat by creating a cool escape. All you need is two plastic pools and little bit of lumber.

Place four four-by-four posts firmly into the ground so that the first pool fits snugly in the center. Nail two two-by-fours to create parallel supports across the insides of two posts. Turn the second pool upside down and use it as a roof.

Fill the bottom pool with water and bubbles and top the roof off with a sprinkler that provides a steady shower.

Fall
Leaf-Pile Lodge

Reward your kids for raking up leaves by converting the pile into a private hideaway with the help of a single large box. Cut a wide three-sided flap, then prop the flap up with some sticks. Let it serve as both a front door and an awning. Pile leaves and debris around the box until the entire structure is covered. When the fun ends, push everything into the box and cart it off to the trash.

POP TEN LIST
Ten Quick-and-Easy Indoor Forts

1. Bedside Manor—Stretch a sheet between the bed and the top drawer of a dresser. Line the floor with pillows, store snacks in the bottom drawers, and place reading materials under the bed.

2. Bunk Bed Bunker—Tuck one end of a sheet under the top mattress and the other end under the bottom mattress. Run sheets side by side until you cover the lower bunk completely.

3. Chair Chamber—Space four chairs at the corners of an imaginary square. Point the seats of the chairs in so your child can use them as shelves. Drape a sheet over the backs so your child can hide underneath.

4. Chaise "Lounge"—Turn porch chairs on their sides and have your kids camp out in the middle. Run long beach towels across the top to create a roof.

5. Clothes Quarters—Clean out the floor of a closet so your child has a cubbyhole beneath the hanging clothes. Place silk plants in front of the open door to camouflage the entrance.

6. Couch Cave—Reposition the cushions. Stand them on their sides or lay them between the couch and the coffee table until your child has a comfortable place to hide. You may even find some loose change or that lost TV remote in the process.

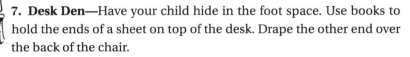

7. Desk Den—Have your child hide in the foot space. Use books to hold the ends of a sheet on top of the desk. Drape the other end over the back of the chair.

8. Pillow Palace—Grab every pillow and removable cushion in the house. Pile them high, crawl inside, and you live in complete comfort (even if it collapses).

9. Room with a View—Angle curtains away from the walls by draping the bottoms over the backs of heavy chairs. Let your child settle in behind them.

10. Table Tent—Drape big blankets over the top of a table so your child can hide underneath. Create additional living space by pulling out the chairs, reversing them, and draping the ends of the blanket over the backs.

For more ideas on inside forts, see Chapter 6: Thinking Outside the Box.

6
Thinking Outside the Box
Clever Cardboard Creations

Kids have a strange connection to cardboard. A big box that once held an appliance can hold a child's attention for hours. The Amazing Dad understands why: An empty box is full of possibilities.

Awesome Auto

Turn a box on its side. Cut an opening in the top leaving a flap hanging down for a dashboard. Decorate the dash with buttons or markers and add a steering wheel made from a paper plate fastened with a brad.

Glue paper plates on for tires, then use art supplies to create headlights, doors, and other desired features. Use chairs for front seats and wedge a paper-towel roll between them for a gearshift. Let your child drive while a stuffed friend rides shotgun. Backseats (and backseat drivers) are optional.

Big Screen TV Set

Cut a window to represent the screen. Use markers or buttons to add knobs, then cut a flap in the back so your kids can crawl in and out of the set. Make yourself a cardboard remote control, then channel surf as your kids make fake news reports, reenact their favorite shows, or create programs of their own.

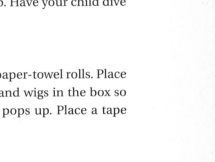

Easy-Make Oven

Draw four round burners on the top of a box, then cut a door on the side for baking. Place a child's chair inside for an oven shelf. Who knows what your kids will cook up?

Funny Fish Tank

Paint the inside of a box to resemble water, then cut a window in a side. Fasten construction paper fish to some string, then hang them through holes in the top. Have your child dive in, pretending to be a scuba diver, a mermaid, or a sea monster.

Jack in the Box

Decorate the sides in various colors, then add a crank made out of paper-towel rolls. Place your kid inside and gently close the flaps. Keep a stash of funny hats and wigs in the box so your child can make a quick change and surprise you each time she pops up. Place a tape player inside to provide a little "pop" music.

Perfect Playhouse

Cut doors and windows, then tape the top flaps up to form a roof. Decorate the walls of the house with art supplies, stickers, or wrapping paper. Furnish the inside with smaller boxes serving as furniture or appliances. Draw and hang a few pictures on the inside walls, and your kid will have a home away from home right there in your home!

Perfect Workplace

For career-minded kids, customize a playhouse to create a storefront, fire station, or ever-present cubicle. Just be ready to do some redesigning when your kid decides to change jobs or gets a promotion.

Royal Palace

Draw a pattern of big stones on the outside walls, then cut tall, thin windows. Create a drawbridge by making a three-sided flap that opens from the top and lies flat on the floor. Tie a string to the back of the flap so it can be pulled shut from inside. Design a family flag and fly it from a lookout tower made from a smaller box.

Super Computer

Draw buttons, levers, and lights all over the outside. Attach objects to manipulate. Add buttons to press, switches to flip, and an old calculator to punch in the information. Use paper plates and brads for spinning wheels and a roll of paper towels for a printout. Hide in the box with paper and pen. Write answers to your kid's questions, and slip your responses through a selected slot.

Note: Use these same ideas with smaller boxes so your kids can use the creations with their toys.

7

Snow Business

A Flurry of Frozen Fun

You've made snow angels. You've thrown snowballs. You've caught snowflakes on your tongue. It's been nice, but your kids' attentions are beginning to drift.
Don't leave them out in the cold. Get down to business and create some snowy surprises that are sure to warm their hearts.

Walkie-Talkie Snowman

Wouldn't you love to build a frosty snowman who can walk and talk? We're still working on the walking part, but we've got the talking part down pat.

Wrap a walkie-talkie in your snowman's scarf, or place one under his hat. Hide nearby and speak to anyone who comes along. Strike up conversations: "Nice weather we're having." Ask questions: "Pardon me, do you have the temperature?" Hand out compliments: "Nice legs. Wish I had some."

For a lower-tech, but equally talkative, snowman, speak into the end of a garden hose that runs through the snowman's body and out of his mouth.

Handstand Snowman

Construct a three-level snowman that turns heads by standing on his.

Begin by forming the snowman's head and adding facial features. When complete, set it upside down on the ground. Make the second level of the snowman slightly wider, adding two arms that run to the

25

ground for support. Build the top level roughly the same size as the second. Place two boots with the bottoms sticking up into the air.

AMAZING DAD MOMENT
Unpredictable Footprints

A few winters back, my son and I hatched a plot to have fun with our neighbors. I cut a pair of monster-sized feet from plywood and fastened them to my boots. We stayed up one snowy evening waiting for everyone to fall asleep.

I placed my son atop my shoulders and pulled on the boots. With his creative navigation and my long strides, we left a pattern of widely spaced, deeply set footprints through the front yards of nearby houses. We warmed up with a cup of hot chocolate, went to bed, and slept late as the neighborhood awoke and made the surprising discovery.

We have repeated the prank, one evening only, for three winters in a row. We plan to keep going until someone figures out our monstrous scheme.

Blocks of Ice

Create the coolest set of blocks your kid has ever seen. Find a variety of disposable, open-faced containers (pudding cups, egg cartons, juice boxes with the tops cut off). Fill them with water, set them outside during the next freeze, and let them harden into shape.

Cut away and dispose of the containers, then begin building. Stack the slippery shapes on top of each other or drip a bit of water between them so they freeze together. The blocks of ice will provide guaranteed solid fun . . . at least until they melt.

Close-up Snowflakes

WHAT YOU'LL NEED: One sheet of black construction • A magnifying glass • Snowflakes

Get a view of a perfectly intact, one-of-a-kind, delicate miracle of nature! Here's a surprisingly easy way to do it: Keep a sheet of black construction paper in your freezer until there is a good snowfall. Take the paper outside, let some snowflakes land on it, then quickly view them through a magnifying glass.

Since flakes are so fragile, you and your child will see a lot of beautifully shattered fragments scattered across the page. Don't give up! Keep catching and viewing. You'll soon discover a special snowflake that survived the impact to give you a fleeting glimpse of its glory.

Snow Ice Cream

Fix a quick and tasty frozen treat! All the ingredients you need except for the snow should be sitting in your kitchen. (If the snow is sitting in your kitchen, forget the recipe and fix the roof.) Begin by gathering these ingredients:

1 cup sweetened condensed milk
1½ cups whole milk
1½ teaspoons vanilla extract
½ cup sugar
8 cups clean, fresh-fallen snow
Various toppings (sprinkles, chocolate syrup, cherries, etc.)

To get the freshest snow possible, put a clean pan outside during a good snowfall. Set it in a place where it will be not be bothered by car fumes or animals. Bring it in when you have gathered enough.

Mix all of the ingredients in a big bowl, adding the snow last. If the ice cream doesn't seem thick enough, just add a little extra snow. Scoop individual servings into bowls. Have a supply of chocolate syrup, maraschino cherries, and colorful sprinkles so everyone can decorate and flavor the ice cream in their favorite style.

Writing in the Snow

Write in the snow without setting a bad example! Fill squeeze bottles with water and food coloring. Draw pictures, write messages, and play games.

Mr. Sandman

Building Excitement at the Beach

A trip to the beach is just what you *make* of it. So make something cool! Break barriers and go beyond castle walls to create adventures your kids are sure to dig.

Beach Volcano

Making a volcano from plaster or clay is a classic activity that scares off even the most daring dads. Most fathers fear the same scenario: the messy construction will destroy the home and mom will be the only thing that blows a top.

For a safe and easy way to brave a volcano, take a few supplies to the beach and construct a "natural" disaster right on the shore. Make a thick mountain in hard sand, tunnel out the center, and set a plastic cup inside. Create flowing lava by adding these beach-safe ingredients (in order):

1 tablespoon baking soda.
1 or 2 drops red food coloring (for a hot, lavalike look)
¼ cup vinegar

Stand back as the volcano becomes active and watch your kids erupt with excitement.

Repeat the process as many times as your supplies allow, then pick up all the bags or containers. Don't forget the plastic cup! Leave the remains of your volcano to wash out to sea.

Daddy Mummy

Lie flat on your back with your arms folded across your chest. Close your eyes, keep perfectly still, and let your kids pile sand over your body. When you are nearly covered, surprise the kids by awakening suddenly in your tomb. Rise from the earth and chase them around "mummy" style.

DUH (Dad's Useful Hints): Sneak an occasional peek while you are being buried. If the kids get too wrapped up in the whole mummy concept, you may get in over your head.

Save the Soldier/Protect the Princess

Carry a plastic character to a spot on the shore that stays dry for a minute or so between waves. Build a quick mound, set the toy on top, and then work quickly with your child to save the toy from the next wave. Dig moats, build walls, or form canals to lead water in the wrong direction.

When a wave comes, stand back and watch. (Diving sideways in front of the structure is a splashy, but illegal, move.) If the water knocks the toy over, grab it so it is not taken out to sea and begin again a few steps back. If the character remains standing, repair structural damage and await another wave. See how long you can maintain the safe haven.

VARIATIONS: Try keeping two characters standing in separate structures. Work together or compete to see who has the better success.

Quicksand

Stand on the shore and dig with your toes every time a wave rushes over your feet. Each time the tide goes out, you will be a little deeper under the sand.

DUH (Dad's Useful Hints): It's cool to act crazy to impress the kids, but if your chin reaches the water, you've sunk too low.

1. **An Animal Sculpture**—A sleeping dragon, a beached whale, a sandy-lion.

2. **A City**—Multiple structures of varying heights with roads running through. Give it a clever name like Sandy-eggo or Wetropolis.

3. **A Fort**—Square walls with towers at each corner and something important protected inside (toys, shells, maybe even Mom).

4. **A Maze**—A path of walls and passageways for toy people to wander through.

5. **A Mermaid**—Bury your child's legs under a pile of sand, then sculpt the pile to look like a fish tale.

6. **A Person**—A humorous head looking up from the sand or a "sandman" (think "snowman" without the cold weather).

7. **Pyramids**—Mountains with smooth, triangular sides and a sphinx standing guard.

8. **A Roller Coaster**—A tall, sturdy tower with roads for a small ball to roll down.

9. **A Ship**—A basic ark shape or a front-half angled up as if sunken in the sand.

10. **A UFO**—A saucer and aliens decorated with seaweed, shells, or debris.

9
A Treasured Memory

An Enchanting Quest for a Pirate's Chest

Have you ever dreamed of finding a message in a bottle or discovering a pirate's treasure? Your kid probably has. You can fulfill those dreams and share in the adventure. We've got the whole thing mapped out for you!

How to Set It Up

1. Create a Treasure Chest

Find something to serve as a treasure chest. Any of these will work great:

a cigar box • an old jewelry box • a tackle box • a mason jar • a lunch box

If you use a kid's lunch box, paint over the pictures, or invent a story to connect the pictures to pirates. ("Pirates used to ride these silly ponies to the ends of these pretty rainbows to search for pots of gold!")

2. Fill the Treasure Chest

Fill the chest with small objects that are fun for your child and safe for the beach. Start with these and add ideas of your own.

jewelry (costume stuff or Mom's discards) • coins (foreign ones!) • game room tokens • colorful rocks • snacks • toys and trinkets

3. Load the Map

We've drawn a map for you. All you have to do is make it look like it belonged to a real pirate. Photocopy the map onto parchment paper, add tea stains, and burn the edges so it appears as authentic as possible. (Pirates were famous for sparking fires and spilling beverages while using their copy machines!) The map is guaranteed to lead you to a treasure every time, as long as you remember where the treasure is buried. To print a special, color version of the map, please visit our web site at www.amazingdad.com.

Roll up the map, tie a string around it, and get an empty wine bottle. (We couldn't find a way to include the bottle with the book so you'll have to empty one of your own! Peel off the labels when you are done.) Slide the map into the bottle and run the string out of the top. This will make the map easier to pull out. Put the cork on the bottle and you are ready to go!

How to Pull It Off

1. Get the Stuff to the Beach

Hide the box and the bottle anywhere your kid won't notice, in a beach bag, in a folding chair, wrapped in a stack of towels.

2. Bury the Treasure

Have mom distract your kids. They can play in the water, search for shells, or retrieve something you "accidentally" left in the car. Dig a deep hole, bury the box, and make an *X* to mark the spot. Use seaweed, shells, or just draw it in the sand.

Cover the *X* with a beach blanket, a towel, or a chair. Sit back and put on your best poker face (and some sunscreen).

3. Float the Bottle

While your kid is playing safely in the water, secretly sneak the bottle down to the shore. Conceal it under a towel that's draped around your neck, or hide it in the back of your bathing suit. Slip into the water. When your kid isn't watching, release the bottle so he or she can discover it. If you are caught holding it, explain that you just picked it up and were wondering what it was. Let your child notice the paper inside.

You hold in your hands a most magical note.
That I placed in a bottle to keep it afloat.
It has traveled for miles by wind and by wave
Avoiding all strangers not honest and brave.
It has sailed straight to you and that means you must
Be someone an old pirate captain can trust.
I'm stranded on an island and I cannot reach
The treasure I buried long ago on your beach.
It's no good to me now at the age I have grown
So I bequeath it to you to keep as your own.
Begin your adventure at the sketch for the sword
Then follow the map to claim your reward.

Step One is a clever and challenging chore
Put your heels in the water and your toes on the shore.

Now look to your shadow, find where it faces,
Then crab crawl sideways for twenty-two paces.

Choose a longitude line, then move perpendicular
To the parallel latitude line in particular.

Find the horizon and look to the tides
With your eyes facing seaward, take ten backward strides.

Lie on your back, take a breath of fresh air,
Rest your bones for a moment, you're just about there.

Now rise like the sun, feel for the breeze,
And skip sixteen steps at 60 degrees.

Walk in a spiral from the spot where you stand,
And you'll find the treasure 'neath the X in the sand.

4. Begin the Quest

Remove the note, read it aloud, then use your knowledge to decipher the deceptively vague instructions. (In other words, go any direction you want!) The strategic design lets you lead your child right to the treasure. The strange descriptions keep you laughing along the way.

5. Uncover the Treasure

The map will lead you to the object you placed on top of the *X*. Your child is likely to look under it. If not, feign disappointment. Pick up the blanket or chair as if ready to go so that you "accidentally" uncover the *X*. Help dig (making sure your child is the one who finds the treasure), then open the box and marvel at the riches it contains.

Pack away the note and bottle when you are ready to go. Make sure not to leave any of the bounty behind. As your child takes home the wonderful reward, you'll take home the wonderful memory, knowing the real treasure is the adventure that the two of you were able to share.

PART III

The Amazing Dad as
Captain Creativity

10
Birthday Mirth
Making Sure Getting Older Never Gets Old

The day of your child's birth brings great joy to your life. Your job is to bring the same great joy to all of your child's birthdays. Mark the passage of time by making each birthday truly special and by finding ways to celebrate throughout the year.

The Birthday Tree

Plant a tree when your child is born. Photograph your kid next to the tree once every birthday. Hang birthday cards from the branches for decorations.

The Birthday Song

Announce to a crowd that you are going to sing "The Birthday Song." Make a big deal of warming up your vocal chords with throat clearing and "Me me me-ing" to give the illusion that you are about to perform a major production number.

Get the whole room clapping a steady beat, encouraging them to sing along whenever they're ready. Ignore protests of "we don't know the words" and begin the song with an incredible burst of enthusiasm.

(Singing to the tune of "Ta Ra Ra Boom De Ay.")
(Slowly at first) **This . . . is . . . your *(quicker)* birthday song!**
It isn't very long!

37

Stop suddenly on the last word and walk away, leaving the crowd surprised and chuckling. **A MUSICAL NOTE:** If your kid is a ham, rehearse "The Birthday Song" together and perform it as a duet at parties you attend.

Pepperoni Pizza Surprise

Next time you order pizza for your kid's birthday party, ask the chef to place the pepperonis in the shape of your child's age.

AMAZING DAD MOMENT
The Most Popular Kid in the World

The week before my daughter turned ten, I contacted as many relatives, friends, and business associates as I could. I gave them the date of my daughter's birthday and asked each of them to call my home between the hours of ten and twelve.

My daughter felt like a queen as she received an endless string of "happy birthday" wishes and still had a smile on her face when her friends began arriving for her party at two.

Birthday Fractions

Kids may fear fractions in math class, but they eagerly apply them whenever announcing their age. ("I'm four and a half!" "I'm seven and three quarters.") Why not take their enthusiasm and expand it?

Quarters for Quarters

Mark your kid's quarter birthdays on the calendar. There are two of them. (Technically, there are four, but who's counting?)

When your kid turns three and a quarter years old, give her three dollar bills and a quarter. Six months later, when she turns three and three quarter years old, adjust the amount accordingly.

The payments increase nicely along with your child's understanding and appreciation of finances, and the quarter-birthday concept is usually abandoned before it will ever force you to go broke.

DUH (Dad's Useful Hint): If you are counting cash because your kid reminds you that he is twenty-nine and three quarters, you've been had.

The Half-Birthday Party

Throw a party on your child's half-birthday (exactly six months after the last birthday: exactly six months before the next). Go all out by doing everything halfway!

Invitations: Create homemade invitations. Cut them down the middle. Deliver them in half-envelopes. (Be sure to include complete directions or your guests will only make it to the halfway point!)

Gifts: Encourage guests to bring half-presents (half a pair of socks) or to divide a serious gift and present each half separately.

Decorations: Divide and conquer as many things as you can. Create half-birthday hats. Hang half a banner. Fill half-a-piñata half-full with candy bars cut in half! Can't cut the balloons? Simply blow them up halfway.

Candles: Buy a candle in the shape of a number. Cut the top half off so it will still light. A five-year old's candle should be half a six since he's halfway there.

Food: Serving half the food can be twice the fun. Bake half a cake, or serve cupcakes cut in two. Cook half–hot dogs on half a bun. Cut soft cones in half from top to bottom, turn them sideways, and add a half scoop of ice cream.

Activities: Sing half of "Happy Birthday." Pin half a tail on half a donkey. Stop the party halfway through and have a halftime celebration.

DUH (Dad's Useful Hint): Playing pin the tail on the donkey with half a blindfold will not work.

Be creative and crazy and your child is sure to "half" a good time!

11
Flashy Photographer
Suggestions for Snappy Snapshots

If a picture is worth a thousand words, imagine the value of a camera full of film. Introduce your kid to photography, and you'll develop creativity, a sense of history, and some pretty nifty pictures.

"Cheese" Substitutes

Look through a lens, ask a kid to say "cheese," and what do you get? The movement of mouth muscles to synthetically simulate a grin. Not exactly a Kodak moment. If you've noticed "cheese" becoming a bit stale, surprise your kid with the unexpected, and get a genuine smile.

FORMAGE!

What to say instead of "cheese":

Rhyming words: Peas! Knees! Fleas!

Crazy combos: Liver Jell-O! Fuzzy pickle! Eeny weeny jelly beanie!

Nutty names: Kirby Shankerbean! Tinky Winky! Soupy Sales!

Wacky words: Onomatopoeia! Wookyhoo! Nerkle!

You know what makes your kid smile. Use your knowledge and get photographic proof of how happy you can make them.

Picture in a Picture in a Picture

Create an amazing photographic image of your kid holding a picture of himself holding a picture of himself holding a picture. Follow these steps:

Take picture # 1: A close-up of your son. Develop it.

Take picture # 2: A close-up of your son holding picture #1. Develop it.

Take picture # 3: A close-up of your son holding picture #2. Develop it.

Follow the pattern until you run out of patience (or film).

You can create this image quickly with an instant or digital camera, or turn it into something truly special by taking the photos at one-year intervals (every birthday, every New Year's Eve, the first day of each school year).

Camera Scavenger Hunt

Make a list of interesting items and cool places around the neighborhood, then combine the ideas to create photos that can be completed for points.

Here's a sample: A photo of a kid wearing a football helmet sitting on a bike holding a teddy bear. Bonus points for every type of ball included in the photo.

Set a few rules (how far they can travel, when to return), then supervise their efforts. Alert other parents to do the same if a search party suddenly shows up at their house. Award five points for each item clearly visible in a photo, then let the kids create a souvenir scrapbook.

Photo Comic Book

Here's a fun way to use a camera to create a book. Help your kid plan a story (an adventure, a romance, a parody of a movie or fairy tale), then illustrate it by posing toys and taking pictures of them. Put the pictures in a scrapbook, write a short caption for each, then show it off to your friends and family. If it is a success, start work on a sequel.

VARIATION: Instead of toys, create comic books featuring family members, friends, or household pets.

AMAZING DAD MOMENT
The Adventures of Skippy

Skippy is a tacky ceramic clown my father had since childhood. When Mom took it from his den and put it in her garage sale, Dad took it back saying he needed it for sentimental reasons. Mom laughed and said he was just ashamed to admit to our neighbors that he owned it.

Eventually Mom told him to do something with it or throw it out. Dad got inspired and began taking Skippy along with us on family vacations. We took photographs of Skippy in all sorts of exotic places. Skippy on a roller coaster. Skippy at the Statue of Liberty. Skippy with the Yankees at spring training. We even allowed Skippy to take vacations with trusted friends so we could collect photos of him in places we'd never been.

The photo album of his adventures is so funny that Mom now lets Skippy and his scrapbook sit right out on her living room coffee table.

12

Pop's Puppet Primer

What to Use, Where to Perform, and What to Do

Be the life of the party by bringing life to a puppet. These crafty friends will entertain your kids and allow you to play any role you desire. Try your hand at these suggestions. Puppets can be made from virtually anything. To create some of the puppets below you'll need markers, a spoon, your fingers, doll's clothes, a sock with buttons and yarn for a face, an oven mitt, a hat . . . let your imagination run wild!

POP TEN LIST
Ten Things to Use as a Puppet

1. Fingers—Paint faces on the fingerprint side and dress them with doll clothes, paper outfits, or decorative Band-Aids.

2. Fist—Close your hand, fold the tip of your thumb inside, then flap it to create a talking mouth. Add eyes, lips, and an attitude.

3. Hats—Place your hand in a hat and turn it sideways. Convert a blue snow hat into a furry monster, a white chef's cap into a talking cloud, yellow cowboy hat into a smiling sun.

4. Doll—Hold a doll upright by the bottom of its feet and make up a show off the top of your head. If the doll laughs or cries, you've got built-in special effects.

5. Inanimate Objects—Grab an object and give it a voice. Create Larry the Lamp, Irene the Iron, or Pablo the Peanut Butter Sandwich.

6. Odd Socks—Turn odd socks into odder characters. Use markers or buttons to create facial features, and yarn or cotton to create hair.

7. Oven Mitts—Cook up warm and lovable pals with a fluffier and fuller version of a sock puppet.

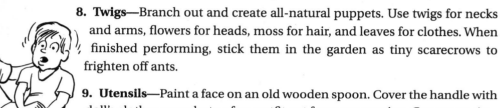

8. Twigs—Branch out and create all-natural puppets. Use twigs for necks and arms, flowers for heads, moss for hair, and leaves for clothes. When finished performing, stick them in the garden as tiny scarecrows to frighten off ants.

9. Utensils—Paint a face on an old wooden spoon. Cover the handle with doll's clothes or a photo of an outfit cut from a magazine. Concoct a similar creature from a fork, or see what you can whip together with an eggbeater.

10. Your Kid—Sit him on your lap like a ventriloquist's dummy, asking him to move his mouth when you tap his neck, or stand above him moving imaginary strings so he can dance like a marionette.

POP TEN LIST
Ten Things to Use for a Performance Space

1. Bag—Place your elbow in a bag. Hold it tight against your side with the puppet peeking out.

2. Big Box—Cut a window at a desired height, then sit or kneel inside.

3. Blanket—Cover yourself with a blanket so only the puppets stick out.

4. Couch—Kneel behind it and put puppets over the top.

5. Chairs—Lay a broom between two chairs, drape a blanket over it, and hide behind.

6. Doorway—Wedge a retractable curtain rod in the doorway, cover it, and play to either room.

7. **Nothing**—Just grab a puppet and go.

8. **Small Box**—Cut a hole in the side and run your hand through so the puppet pops out the top. Hold the box with the other hand or place it on a surface.

9. **Shower Curtain**—Peek puppets through the middle, around the side, or over the top.

10. **Table**—Sit on one side holding the puppet in view or hide under with the puppet peeking out.

POP TEN LIST
Ten Things to Do With Puppets

1. Act out a fairy tale.
2. Create a movie parody.
3. Host a toy talk show.
4. Kiss a kid on the cheek.
5. Launch a tickle attack.
6. Lip-synch a song.
7. Perform an original play.
8. Reenact family adventures.
9. Teach a lesson.
10. Tell a joke.

Sew? What!

Quick and Easy Costumes and Props

The next time your kids want to play dress up, capture their imaginations by using yours. Create anything and everything out of virtually nothing.

Seventeen Outstanding Outfits

Binoculars—Tape two toilet paper rolls side by side. For high-power lenses, use paper towel rolls.

Boots—Have your child step into a paper bag, then twist it around his leg. Decorate with markers to designate whether they are for cowboys, spacemen, or fashion models.

Chef's Hat—Place the open end of a pillow case over your child's forehead. Run it above his ears, wrap the excess in back with a rubber band, then fluff the top into shape.

Crown—Cut the shape from construction paper, decorate, then staple it into the proper size. (**DUH: Dad's Useful Hint:** Do stapling before placing it on your child's head, so she does not end up wearing it permanently.)

Hawaiian Skirt—Cut the top off a paper bag and cut fringe in the bottom. Have your child step into it like a skirt, then use a belt to hold it in place while she hulas.

Indian Vest—Cut a slit up the front of a paper bag. Cut holes for head and arms, then cut strips of fringe at the bottom. Paint designs on the vest and on the face and body of the Indian who wears it.

Karate Uniform—Place your child in one of your old, white work shirts. For a fun belt, use one of your least favorite, but most colorful neckties. (But not the one she gave you last Father's Day!)

Magic Wand—Tape a construction-paper star on the top of a colorful pencil. Decorate with ribbon or glitter to suit fairy godmothers, good fairies, wizards, witches, or warlocks.

Megaphone—Slice the bottom half off a plastic milk jug. Have your child hold the handle and talk through the opening.

Robot—Use a paper bag or medium-sized box. Cut head and arm holes, then decorate with drawings of wires and buttons.

Pointed Cap—Roll newspaper into a tall cone, then tape it together. Decorate to suit a witch, a wizard, a maiden, or a dunce.

Sheriff's Star—Cut a cardboard star, wrap it in tin foil, then tape it to a shirt. Badge may double as a Japanese throwing star for sheriffs who double as ninjas.

Shield—Color the front of a paper plate. Cut a strip from the middle of another. Tape the strip to the back as a handle.

Stethoscope—Attach a plastic butter tub lid or a suction cup to the pronged end of portable radio headphones.

Space Helmet—Cut a hole in the front of a paper bag so that your child's face will poke through. Decorate with crayons or markers.

Telescope—Decorate two paper-towel rolls. Tape them end to end, or slide the first into another with a slightly larger circumference.

Toga—Wrap a folded sheet around your child's waist, then toss the rest over his shoulder. Perfect for portraying emperors, gladiators, and partying college kids.

AMAZING DAD MOMENT
Masquerade Mystery

One night my kids and I rented costumes and went out to eat. Cody was a Star Wars storm trooper, Jocelyn was a flapper, and I had a Wild Wild West thing going with a bowler, ruffled shirt, and little glasses.

Everyone at the restaurant was trying to figure out where we were going. When we told them we were just out to eat, they thought it was great.

As we drove home, a lady pulled up next to us and asked if we were going to a party. When I told her what we were doing, she laughed and told the kids they had the coolest dad in the world. It was a great night that we'll obviously repeat.

14

Pop's Paper Tree

Five Lessons to Grow On

This is one of our favorite things in the book. Give it your all and it will become one of your favorites, too! Fascinate your child with a memorable routine that turns five sheets of newspaper into a towering tree. Add dramatic impact by reciting a poem and using the tree to deliver a special message.

Creating the Paper Tree

Find five double-pages of newspaper and set them in a pile. Roll the first sheet of newspaper into a tube. Stop about five inches from the edge. Add a second double-page sheet and continue rolling, stopping again with about five inches to go. Add the third, fourth, and fifth sheets the same way, rolling the fifth one all the way up to complete the tube.

Flatten the tube, hold the top, and slowly begin to tear a straight line down the center. Tear about an inch at a time, stopping when you are about one third of the way down the tube. Flatten the tube the opposite way (so the torn strips lie on top of each other). Make a second tear down the center just as you did before.

You now have four torn parts made up of several strips. Bend them out from the center like fronds of a palm tree.

Put your fingers into the top of the tube and pull the innermost page upward in one swift motion. The tubes will telescope, stretching the tree to its full length.

Presenting the Poem

The best method of presenting the poem is to simply memorize it and recite it as you make the tree. This is not as hard as it sounds.

There is an opening verse to say as you set out the paper, one verse for each sheet you add, and a final verse to recite as you make the tears. Your actions will help you remember the words and the words will help you remember the actions! Time the presentation so you can stretch the tree to its full length right after reciting the last line.

If you don't think you can learn the entire poem, memorize the first and last verses only. Photocopy the five middle verses and glue one onto each of the five sheets of newspaper. Read the verses as you add each page then roll them out of view.

Whichever method you use, present the poem with passion and panache to deliver an experience your child will never forget!

Five Lessons to Grow On

One day my father came to me with a smile
And showed me five sheets stacked up in a pile.
He told me each sheet represented a seed:
A small grain of knowledge I was going to need.
He took the first sheet and he set it down flat.
He rolled it a bit till it looked just like that.
Then he stopped and shared the first piece of advice,
"Never forget you should always be nice."
As I smiled at his words and started to think,
He grabbed the next sheet and gave me a wink.
He rolled them together combining the two,
And told me, ***"Be honest in all that you do."***
He reached out his hand and picked up the third.
He rolled it the same without saying a word.
Then he looked in my eyes, and the message he gave
Was, ***"Believe in yourself and strive to be brave."***
Next, he reached up and took sheet number four.
He put the page with the rest and rolled them some more.
They all intertwined, and I heard father say,
"Find a reason to laugh in your life every day."
He took the last sheet and he smiled at me.
I was longing to learn what the fifth seed would be.
He rolled the sheet in where the others had gone,
And said, ***"Teach what you know so your knowledge lives on."***
He said, "If you plant these seeds deep in your heart,
You'll always be strong even when we we're apart."
I followed his words and with them I grew.
Now I'm passing my father's knowledge to you.

PART IV

The Amazing Dad as

The Chauffeur of Shenanigans

15
Drive 'Em Crazy
Creating Cheer While You Steer

Put yourself in the driver's seat and turn the family car into a "wheely" fun place to be. Safe and silly surprises are the key to making your next drive a real trip. Here are some great gags and tricks to get you going.

Passenger Horn Prank

Brag about your recent installation of a passenger horn. Explain that you did it for safety reasons, so a passenger can honk in case they see something that you don't. Demonstrate the feature by leaning over to the glove compartment. Press the lock, the logo, or any flat surface and produce an instant honking sound.

The effect is achieved with simple misdirection. As you reach your right hand over to press the glove compartment, your left hand rests upon the steering wheel and secretly honks the horn.

Radio-Controlled Car

As you strap everyone in safely, ad-lib remarks about how the car has been acting crazy lately. Start it up and suggest a little music before you go. Reach over to turn on the radio, secretly starting the windshield wipers at the same time.

Say, "Isn't that crazy? Watch this!" Change the station, secretly speeding up the wipers as soon as you find a fast-paced song. Point and say, "It's like the radio is making them dance!"

Leave the wipers on, then try any or all of these crazy combinations:

Adjust the balance to the right side—lower the windows on the left.

Adjust the balance to the left side—lower the windows on the right.

Adjust the fade to the front—lower the windows in the back.

Adjust the fade to the back—lower the windows in the front.

Fix the sound so all the windows are back up, turn off the radio to stop the wipers, and explain that everything will work fine once the car is moving.

Announce that you are going to lock the doors before you drive off. Reach over, push the lock, and release your seat so it drops into a reclining position. Straighten up, laugh it off, and hit the road.

Red Light/Green Light

Next time you are stuck behind a red light, ask your kid to use a little magic to turn it green.

Take a moment to explain the proper incantation. Teach her a magic poem (*Traffic signal, don't be mean. Turn your light from red to green!*), demonstrate a magic gesture (*a wave of the hand, a snap, and a point*), or pass along a magic word (*Presto Change-o!*).

As you teach her the trick, keep your eyes on the other traffic signals so you know just when your light is about to change. Instruct your child to perform her spell so they coincide perfectly.

Splashy Sneeze

Lean your head back like you are about to sneeze. As you bring it forward with a loud "Achoo!" strike the wiper lever to send a quick burst of washing fluid all over your windshield. With a "Wow! That was a big one!" turn the wipers on and clean off the remains of the sneeze.

Parking Place Prayer

As you circle a parking lot in search of a free space, invite a little divine intervention by reciting this parking place prayer: *Hail Taxi. Full of grace. Deliver us a parking space.*

Recite the words just before reaching a space you have secretly spotted ahead of the kids. Pull right in as if the space were delivered by magic.

AMAZING DAD MOMENT
Magic Lights

As a child, we took many trips to my grandma's house. To maximize our time, Pop would do most of the driving at night. He helped pass the hours with a game he called "Magic Lights."

My brother and I would say the magic words, "Squeegem, Squeegem, little Chick-a-Chak. Let's make music for little Quack Quack," and the headlights would magically flash from normal to bright. We'd repeat the phrase, and the lights would mysteriously return to normal.

Pop never let on that he was changing the beams with a switch by his feet, so my brother and I remained astonished for years.

16
Destination Sensations

Strong Tips for Long Trips

**Long trips can lead to long faces even if you're going some-
where great. When your passengers need a little pick me up,
do something special. Create smiles for miles, and make getting there part of the fun.**

Roving Reporters

Bring along a handheld tape recorder so you and your kid can file funny reports throughout the entire trip.

Do press conferences as the journey begins:

"We're about to drive into the mountains, Dad. Think you can handle it?"
*"Well, Son, I'm not worried about the steep slopes, but I'm a little afraid of the country
music stations we'll be forced to listen to."*

Do play-by-play along the route:

"We're three hours into the trip and we've seen nothing but fields of livestock."
"Holy cow! There's another one!"

Do investigative interviews with strangers in strange places:

"So, do you ever get really weird families in this restaurant?"

"We mean, besides ours?"

The reporting will keep you entertained during the trip. The recordings will keep you entertained for years.

Crazy Challenge List

Create a list of five to ten crazy challenges that you and your child must accomplish before reaching your destination. Tailor the tasks to fit your interests as well as your intended route.

Here are examples of things you might include:

1. We must each try one new soft drink and one new candy bar.

2. We must visit a place with a sign that says *World's Best, World's Biggest,* or *World's Only.*

3. We must stand in a spot where our feet touch two different states.

Remember two rules as you add items to your list: Make sure they are safe, and make sure they are fun.

Treat yourself to something special if you successfully complete the list. Treat yourself even if you don't, so you can laugh about the great time you had trying.

AMAZING DAD MOMENT
Father's Themed Trips

WESTWARD HO!

Whenever we went on a vacation, my father would gather props, music, and food that related to the trip. When we drove to Texas, he bought cowboy hats, played western music, stopped for barbecue, and referred to our car as a covered wagon.

For trips we took more than once (like the eight-hour trek to Aunt Carol's), my sisters and I got to select any theme we wanted. We took African safaris, space missions, and even deep-sea submarine excursions.

1. ABC It: Complete the alphabet by spying letters in order on billboards. Compete to see who can do it first.

2. Best Ever: Call out a category so everyone can announce their vote for the "Best Ever." (Best film ever made, best player in the NFL, or best CD we own.)

3. Double Identity: Everyone adopts a new name (as serious or as silly as they wish), then scores a point each time someone uses their old one.

4. License Plate Lookout: Find plates from all states, find numbers from 1 to 10, or create silly meanings for the letters (RVC could mean Rusty Vehicle Club, Retired Violin Collector, or Really Vicious Child.)

5. My Word: Everyone announces a word, then tries to get others to say it. Players earn a point each time someone says their word, but lose a point if they utter it themselves. Outlaw tiny words (*a, the, and*) and curse words (@#!!).

6. Name Ten: Call out categories and work together to name examples. (Name ten tennis players. Name ten cartoon cats. Name ten kinds of pie.)

7. Name That Song: Tune the radio to find a song. Award one point to the person who names the tune and another to the person who names the artist.

8. Sudden Surprise: Hide a stash of gifts (gum, toys, spare change). Give them out to a kid who says a secret word, sees a chosen car, or spies a certain sign.

9. Twenty Questions: Players try to figure out a secret celebrity with twenty "yes or no" questions. (Is it a male? Is he living? Is he a TV star?)

10. Who Are You: Players create characters based on letters of the alphabet. ("My name is Becky. I'm married to Bartholomew. I have a bullfrog named Bubba. I'm going to Bermuda to buy bologna because I'm a ballerina.")

Traveling Trivia

A Game Show on the Go

There are plenty of products that provide trivia, but the greatest single source of knowledge in the known universe is The Amazing Dad! With a little rehearsal (and minimal research) you can turn a simple car trip into a traveling game show that will keep the kids thinking and smiling at the same time.

The Theme Song

Break up the monotony of a mundane trip by launching into a theme song. Ad-lib a tune off the top of your head or alter one from a classic TV show. (Scat to the beat of *Mission Impossible*, add words to the *Jeopardy* theme, or change the lyrics to *Scooby-Doo*.)

Make sure your theme song grabs everyone's attention and lets them know what's coming next. If the game show becomes a tradition, the kids may even learn your tune and sing along.

The Introduction/Interview

Convert passengers into players by adopting an over-the-top announcer voice and welcoming them to the show. Here's an example:

"Live, from the fabulous front seat of the Martin family minivan, it's time for everybody's favorite game show . . . Who Knows What? I'm your host, Dazzling Danny Martin. Let's meet today's contestants! A thirteen-year-old, high school freshman with dreams of becoming a cheerleader . . . Abby Martin! A ten-year-old soccer star with dreams of dating a cheerleader . . . Alex Martin. And finally, an ex-cheerleader and wonderful mom

whose age will remain unannounced so I will remain unharmed . . . the beautiful Madeline Martin!"

Make small talk with each player, asking silly questions about their personal lives *("So Alexander, I am told you enjoy space travel. Tell us a little about that.")*

The Sound Check

In order for you to identify who is "sounding in," each contestant will have to have a distinctive noise to signify when they know the answer. Ask each contestant to create and demonstrate a sound (a bell, a buzzer, an animal call), then take a moment to make sure you can identify each contestant without having to take your eyes off the road.

The Categories

Pick a few topics you know about (baseball, cartoons, desserts) and select some specifically for your contestants (boy bands, video games, weird relatives).

For a crash course on your kids' tastes, take a quick, pretrip peek at some of their magazines, glance at one of their compact discs, or watch one of their favorite TV shows and take mental notes.

Three to five facts in three to five areas are all you need. You can close out categories or add new ones whenever you like.

The Game

To keep the game (and the car) running smoothly, follow this standard six-step game show format:

1. A player chooses a category.

2. You ask a question, then listen for someone to "sound in."

3. A correct response adds points to a player's total.

4. An incorrect response deducts points.

5. When a player answers incorrectly, other players may buzz in.

6. The one who answers correctly chooses next.

The Points

Points are up to you. Make every question worth the same amount, increase values as you continue in a category, or assign random points whenever necessary. *("You are trailing by two thousand, three hundred and fourteen points, Abby, and amazingly, this question is worth exactly that much!")*

Let the players keep score, in their heads or on paper, so you can concentrate on the road.

The End

The game ends when you run out of questions (or, in the worst-case scenario, when you run out of gas). Let the champion sit shotgun, choose the radio station, or select a place to eat. Give a consolation prize to the runners-up by allowing them to suggest categories for the next game.

18
Good Clean Fun
The Car Wash Carnival

When it comes time to clean the car, use a little creativity to convert the chore into something truly special. Mix the bubbles and water with some splashy surprises and you are bound to have buckets of fun.

The Amazing Mr. Bubblefingers

Step right up and become the Amazing Mr. Bubblefingers: a manly man with delicate hands capable of creating the most fragile object in all of the world!

Form a hoop with your hands by pressing your forefingers and thumbs together. Reach into a soapy bucket so your "hand-made" hoop fills up like a bubble wand. Lift your hands out of the water and begin blowing a steady stream of air into the soap film. Slide your hands over each other to close the hoop and seal off the bubble.

Let your kids try their hands at it, then have a contest to see who can blow the biggest man-made bubble of all.

Madame Too-Suds House of Wax

Dip your hands into the soap bucket, spread suds on your face, and impress your kids with silly imitations of famous figures. Make a tiny goatee for Colonel Sanders, a mustache and crazy hair for Albert Einstein, or a bushy white beard for Santa Claus, Rip Van Winkle, or one of the seven dwarves.

Squirting Gallery

Set a few sponges at strategic points atop the car. Stand a few feet back, squeeze the handle of the hose, and see who can squirt them down in the fastest time. For additional fun, have the kids put on swimming goggles so they can play defense. Let them run back and forth in front of the targets trying to distract the squirter and deflect the water.

Window Fun House

Distort your facial features without the aid of fun-house mirrors! When you find yourself on opposite sides of a car door, take the window of opportunity and make a goofy face against the glass. It's the perfect time to mess up the windows because you are just about to clean them!

Here are a few funny favorites:

PIG FACE: Stick the tip of your nose to the glass. Slide your head down slightly so your nostrils flare upward. Snort while your kid goes hog-wild.

PUFFER FISH: Open your mouth and press your lips to the window. Blow against the glass until your cheeks expand. Widen your eyes as wildly as possible.

SQUISHED MOSQUITO: Press your palms flat against the glass. Push the side of your face tight against the glass between them. Look crushed like a bug who has made sudden impact.

The Homemade Rainbow Finale

Stand with your back to the sun and spray the water so it arcs (like a water rainbow) and falls down in a gentle drizzle. Have your kids stand beside you looking into the falling droplets. Ask them to take a few steps to the left or right until they see a rainbow shining through your self-made rain shower.

Let your kids dart into the water to try and touch the rainbow, then invite them to search for the rainbow's end. Hide some coins ahead of time to serve as a miniature pot of gold (and a reward for all their help).

PART V

The Amazing Dad as
The Amazing Dadini

19

Abra-Kid-Abra

The Amazing Dadini's Marvels and MiniMiracles

This book is full of ways for Dad to do extraordinary things with ordinary objects. Here are a few special tricks with a truly magical touch.

The Uncanny Can
(The Soda Can Through the Tabletop)

WHAT YOU'LL NEED: Soda can (salt shaker or ketchup bottle is fine) • Quarter • Napkins

This classic illusion has a surprise ending guaranteed to startle your kid. It can be performed with a variety of objects (a salt shaker, a drinking glass, even a ketchup bottle.) We've used a can of soda to give the trick a little pop.

The Set-up

Sit directly across from your kid and place a quarter heads up on the table in front of you. Set an unopened can of soda next to it.

Explain to your kid that you are going to make the quarter pass right through the table. Tell him that if you are unable to do it, he can have the whole soda.

The Cover-up

Open three paper napkins and stack them on top of the can. Flatten the napkins along the sides so that you can see the shape of the can, but not the can itself. If you can still see the can, add another napkin. When the can is covered, grip it near the bottom, pinning the napkins in place.

NOTE: Use a can that has not been refrigerated. A cold, wet soda will stick to the napkin, show through, and spoil the trick.

The Slip-up

Place the covered can over the coin. Explain that when the metal can touches the metal coin, it will create a spark of magical friction. Explain that the napkins are there to protect your hand. Recite some magic words with great enthusiasm.

Lift the covered can all the way to the edge of the table, acting stunned to find the coin still on the table. Draw your child's focus to the coin by pointing to it and saying, "Oh that's right. Now I remember! The coin has to be facedown so he can see where he is going!"

As you flip the coin over with your free hand, let the soda slip silently out of the napkins so that it lands in your lap. Bring the napkins forward, holding them so they still retain the shape of the can.

The Switch-up

Place the can-shaped napkins over the coin as if ready to try again. Tell your child that if the quarter doesn't pass through the table this time, he gets the soda for himself.

As soon as you have the napkins in place, lift your free hand high and slam the napkins flat. It will appear that you have smashed the can through the table.

The Wrap-up

As your kid reacts in disbelief, focus your attention on the flattened napkins, oblivious to what you have just done. Lift one of the corners slowly, frowning when you see the coin undisturbed. Say, "I really thought I could do it, but the quarter's still there!" Reach under the table, pretending to lift the soda can off of the floor. Hand it to him and say, "You win!"

Now You See It, Now You Don't (The Instant Vanish)

Surprise your kids by selecting something and suddenly making it disappear. With a little misdirection, you can vanish a baseball cap, a Barbie doll, even a banana.

DUH (Dad's Useful Hints): The thing doesn't have to begin with the letter *B*, but it does have to be light enough for you to hold. In other words, we're not teaching you to vanish the Buick.

Begin by taking the object into your left hand and turning your left shoulder toward your child. Pull your left arm back as if you are going to throw the object like a Frisbee. Bring the arm forward and back a couple of times, looking past your child like you are trying to figure out where the object is going to land.

When you bring the object back a third time, secretly pin it under your right arm, then thrust your left arm forward. Extend your fingers as if you have thrown the object, then turn your head to follow its imaginary trajectory. (For a variation, prepare to toss an object straight up, then pin it between your knees.)

When the object vanishes, act as though you are trying to figure out where it has gone. As you look around, simply reposition your body to keep the object hidden from your child's view. To make it reappear, wait for your kid to turn away, grab the object from under your arm, and pretend to pluck it back from the air.

NOTE: Be sure to try the instant vanish with the family dog. (To fool him, not to make him disappear!)

The Bear from a Bare Box (An Amazing, Stuffed Animal Appearance)

This trick will allow you to produce a stuffed animal from a box you have just shown to be empty. It's the perfect way to present your child with a new toy, return something that was believed to be lost, or to reveal an object you have previously made disappear.

WHAT YOU'LL NEED: An empty office-supply box • A three-inch piece of string • A bulldog clip • A stapler • The bear or other toy that you want to make appear

Readying the Trick

Tie a knot in one end of the string, then staple it to the upper inside lip of the lid. Tie the bulldog clip to the loose end of the string, then clip it onto the bear.

Lift the lid into the air for a moment to make sure everything stays together. If the stapled string and the bulldog clip support the weight of the bear, you are all set. (If it falls apart, you'll need to reinforce the string, get a bigger clip, or choose a lighter toy.)

When you are ready to go, place the lid on the box so the bear is resting inside.

Removing the Lid

Stand at one end of a table directly across from your kid. Make sure the stapled end of the box is toward you. Place a light pencil mark on this side so you always know which end is which. Lift and raise your end of the lid with your right hand. Bring the lid up vertically so that the bear dangles unseen behind it.

Draw your child's attention to the box by tilting it upward with your left hand so your child can look inside. At the same time, set the lid down on your end of the table so the string dangles the bear over the edge and out of view.

Replacing the Lid

Act surprised when your child tells you that the box is empty. Look inside the box for a moment, then pretend to remember something. Point at your child with your left hand and tell her to think of a magic word. As you do, use your right hand to lift the lid from the table in the same method as before. Raise it vertically. Keep the bear hidden by tilting the far end of the lid down toward your child as you bring the lid over the box. Guide the object safely inside, then set the lid in place, far end first.

Rotating the Box

Ask your child to tap her end of the box two times while reciting her magic words. When she does, rotate the box 180 degrees and have her do the same to the opposite side. The stapled side of the lid is now facing your child. This allows you to lift your end without disturbing the bear.

Revealing the Surprise

Peek in as if checking to see if the magic words have worked. Smile at your child and tell her that she is not going to believe it. Raise your end of the lid with one hand. Reach into the box with your other hand and unclip the bear. Present it to your child with a flourish and let the lid fall back in place. Be patient as your child hugs her new friend: you'll be hugged next!

Tie 'Em in Stitches (A Magical Tie Routine)

Ties have never been particularly fun. Your kid gives you one on Father's Day, it waits quietly in the closet, then hangs from your neck doing nothing. (It occasionally clashes with your shirt, but even this is boring.)

You can put an end to tie tedium with this crazy routine. Perform it for your kid before heading off to work in the morning and leave him with a smile on his face.

Part One: The Breakfast Breath Test

After having breakfast with your child, lean forward to kiss your kid good-bye. Stop suddenly as if something is wrong, then tell your child that you need to give him "The Breakfast Breath Test."

Lift and hold your tie so that the point faces up and the lining is toward you. Ask your kid to blow on it. As soon as he does, pull the lining downward with your thumb. It will look like the tie is withering from your child's breath. It's a great way to get him to brush his teeth.

Part Two: The Silly String Along

When your child has brushed, administer the "Breakfast Breath Test" a second time and let him pass. Instead of withering the tie, pretend to notice a small string sticking out from the tip. With a slight grimace, lower the tie to normal position, then grip it about six inches up from the end with your thumb in view and your index finger hidden behind.

With your other hand, reach for the tip and pretend to pull the imaginary thread straight out. As you do, flutter the tie by rapidly hitting it from underneath with the middle finger.

Make it look as real as possible. Pull the "thread" a few inches, let it go, then reach to the tip and grab it again. Stop the fluttering each time you pause the pulling. End the pantomime by going through the motions of breaking off the thread, creating the proper sound by snapping your thumbnails together.

Part Three: The Funny Finger Stitch

Wrap up the routine by threading the imaginary string through an invisible needle and pretending to sew your fingers together.

Run the needle through the side of your pinky, playfully wincing as you do. Next, push it through the side of your ring finger. Lift the thread to pull the ring finger and pinky together. Continue the sewing action until all of your fingers are threaded tightly. Hold your hand up, pull the needle end of your invisible thread so your fingers bend and wave good-bye.

20

Presto Change-Oh

The Amazing Dadini's Money Magic

Money magic pays big dividends: it buys you hours of entertainment without costing you a cent. A short time spent practicing will earn you the applause you so richly deserve. Mastering a few coin tricks will peak your kids' interest and make their lives a little richer. (You can bank on it!)

Classic Coin Vanish

Vanishing coins (and other small objects) is an essential skill that all Amazing Dads should possess. An easy and deceptive method to master is the magician's French Drop.

Begin with a coin between the thumb and the middle finger of your right hand. Reach for the coin with your left hand, positioning your left thumb under the coin. Close your left fingers around the coin. Pretend to grab it, but secretly drop it into your right hand.

Clench your left hand as if holding the coin and move it away. Draw focus to the left hand by looking at it. At the same time, curl your right hand to conceal the coin and point a finger toward your left hand. Roll the fingers of your left hand open to show that the coin has vanished.

Astounding Coin Appearances

Hide a coin in your hand. (Use a French Drop or simply sneak one out of your pocket when your kid isn't looking.) Make the coin appear with any of these methods:

Coin from the Air: Reach the hand upward using the thumb to slide the coin from your palm to the tip of your fingers. Do it quickly and smoothly so you appear to pluck the coin from thin air.

Coin from the Ear: Look at your child's ear as if seeing something unusual. Gently tug on his lobe as if plucking something out. Slide the coin to the tips of your fingers then bring it into view.

Coin from the Nose: Conceal the coin in your fist. Turn the hand palm down and playfully pinch your child's nose between your thumb and index finger. Drop the coin from your fist so it appears to fall from the nose. Catch the coin in the other hand.

AMAZING DAD MOMENT
Grandpa Silver

When I was a child, my grandfather showed me my very first coin trick. He rolled up his sleeves, showed his hands unmistakably empty, then reached behind my ear and produced a silver coin.

I became a professional magician later in life and studied the art of magic. I learned its subtleties and misdirection, but the one trick that went without explanation was my grandfather's silver coin production.

Years later, at a family party, I saw my grandfather perform the trick for my little

---

cousin and finally discovered the secret. As grandpa reached his empty hand forward, my grandmother snuck up behind my cousin, slipped a coin into grandpa's hand, then scurried into the next room undetected.

Grandpa produced the silver coin for my spellbound cousin, just as he had done for me . . . with the silent help of Grandma, his lifelong love and secret assistant.

Guess Which Hand

WHAT YOU'LL NEED: Two pennies

Defy the laws of chance with this baffling version of the popular guessing game. The odds appear to be fifty-fifty, but you win one hundred percent of the time.

Pinch a penny between the thumb and index finger of your left hand, secretly clasping a second penny in the fingers below. Reach your right hand over and grab the visible penny as quickly as you can. Turn both fists palm down and ask your child to "Guess Which Hand" holds the coin.

If she points to your left hand, open your right one and reveal the penny. If she points to your right hand, reveal the penny in your left.

In either case, grab the coin with the thumb and index finger of the opposite hand. This allows you to begin again with one penny visible and the other secretly hidden in your fingers below.

Your child will guess wrong indefinitely, or until she figures out you have two coins. For a fun variation, reverse the theme and let her win every time.

Pocket Change

WHAT YOU'LL NEED: Two quarters

Kids are constantly making money disappear out of your pockets. Here's a chance to change things around and put money back in.

Start with a quarter in your left hand. Place the coin flat on your left thigh directly on top of another quarter you have hidden in your pocket.

Pinch a fold of fabric with your left hand so you are holding both quarters together tightly. Fold them upward together, keeping your left thumb on the outside quarter. Make a second upward fold with your right hand. As you do, use your left thumb to secretly slide the outside quarter into your left hand.

Hold the folds toward your child and ask him to pinch and hold the quarter. He will have no idea that he is pinching a quarter that is already in your pocket.

Grab your pants above and below the folds. Yank the fabric in opposite directions so your child loses his grip and the coin "vanishes." Reach your left hand into your left pocket and produce the coin which was hidden in your hand.

The Fast Fling

WHAT YOU'LL NEED: Four dimes

Prove that the hand is quicker than the eye with this clever charade that will have you flinging a coin at the speed of light. To begin, find two hands (yours), two eyes (your kid's), and four dimes (anyone's).

Have your child place one dime in each of your palms. Close your fists and ask your child to place a dime on the fingertips of each of your hands. Hold your fists over a table. Explain that you are going to fling a dime from one hand to the other. Bet your child that she will not be able to see you do it.

Turn your hands toward each other quickly, letting two dimes fall to the table. Pretend as though you have messed up. Your child will believe you have dropped the two coins that were sitting atop your fingertips. Your child will be wrong.

Let's look at the Fast Fling in slow motion to see what really happened. As you turned your left wrist, you let the dime on your left fingertips slip into your palm. As you turned your left wrist, you let both coins fall to the table. The movement of your fingers was so fast that your child was unable to tell.

Shake your head at your failed attempt, then ask your child to take the dimes from the table and place them back on your fingertips. When she does, turn your hands quickly again. Let both dimes slip from the fingertips into the same palms.

Turn the hands back over and open your fingers. You'll have three dimes in your left hand and only one in the right. And your child never saw you do it!

The Card and Coin Challenge

WHAT YOU'LL NEED: One playing card • One quarter

This stunt could have gone in the card chapter or the coin chapter. It's so cool that we could have included it in both!

Hold a hand palm up with your index finger extended. Balance a playing card on the top of the finger. (This isn't the cool part, but it is still pretty neat!)

Place a quarter in the middle of the balanced card, directly over the ball of your finger. Tell your kid that you can remove the card without touching or dropping the coin. Wait for them to express doubt, then go for it.

Flick the card sharply with your middle finger. The card will fly away and the coin will remain in place.

DUH (Dad's Useful Hints): That was the cool part. Be sure to flick the card away from your child, and not into her, so she is able to see it.

21
What a Card
The Amazing Dadini's Coolest Card Tricks

If asked to perform a card trick, most dads can bluff their way through at least one before drawing a blank. The Amazing Dad, on the other hand, knows a great deal of dazzling tricks. He has practiced and perfected them all. Draw from one of these ideas and make your card tricks a cut above the rest.

The Card Force

Knowing in advance which card your kids will select will give you endless magical possibilities. You can control the card your child picks with this simply deceptive method.

Begin by placing the card you want to force on the bottom of the deck. Do not let your child see it. Put the deck in your left hand. Place your right fingers on top of the deck. Place your right thumb under the deck so it is pressing against the preselected card.

Use your middle finger and thumb to pull the top and bottom cards back about an inch each. Move both cards at the same time, keeping the movement of the bottom card hidden from your kid's view. Continue sliding top cards back one at a time with your middle finger. Ask your child to tell you when to stop. When he does, slide the pulled-back cards straight off the back of the deck secretly bringing the bottom "force" card with it.

Hold the deck up without looking and show your child his "freely" selected card. Place the upper half of the deck on top of the lower so his card is buried in the middle. Shuffle the deck so his card is completely lost in the mix. (But not in your mind!)

The force is with you. Go forth and astonish, revealing the card in creative and clever ways.

Revelation One: The Mind Meld

Ask your child to concentrate on his card. Stare deep into his eyes as if you are looking directly into his brain. Raise your eyebrows as if receiving a signal, then announce the color of the card. *"It's . . . Black!"* Continue the act, staring intensely until you have revealed the suit and, ultimately, the value. *"It's . . . a club! It's . . . a seven! It's the seven of clubs!"*

Revelation Two: Fifty-One Card Pickup

Look through the deck, rearranging a few of them as if searching for your child's card. When you come across it, sneak it to the bottom of the deck. Continue searching, then smile as though you have remembered a special method of finding it.

Ask your child to hold the cards tightly, keeping the deck facedown between his thumb and index finger. Strike the deck sharply with your middle and index fingers so all the cards except for one fall to the ground. When your child looks at his hand, he will discover that he is holding his selected card. When he looks at the floor, he will discover he has a mess to clean up. Smile and tell him that it could have been worse. You could have made him pick up all 52!

Revelation Three: The Erased Message

Here's a clever one in which a credibly incomplete answer becomes a completely incredible one.

Take a pencil and write this exact message lightly on a scrap of paper:

THE NAME
OF
THE CARD IS

Fold the paper, then set it on a table in front of your child.

Take a deck of cards and force the ten of hearts. When your child has placed her card back into the deck, ask her to read the prediction you've written on the scrap of paper. When you hear what she reads, grab the paper and explain that you forget to finish it. Reach for the pencil quickly, "accidentally" breaking the lead so you cannot write. Flip the pencil to the eraser side and complete these steps:

1. Erase the *H* in the first *THE*.

2. Erase the *AME* in *NAME*.

3. Erase the *T* in the second *THE*.

4. Erase the *C* and *D* in *CARD*.

5. Erase the bottom of the *I* in *IS* so it looks like a *T*.

Set the pencil down, refold the paper, and ask your child what her card was. When she tells you, ask her to open the paper. As she does, she will discover that the prediction now reads:

TE N
OF
HE AR TS

The Card Beneath the Tablecloth

This astonishing trick is the perfect after-dinner treat. Whet your child's appetite by allowing him to select a card, then use common table items to make it dramatically appear in an unpredictable and impossible place.

WHAT YOU'LL NEED: A white, fabric tablecloth • A glass of water • A spoon • A deck of cards • A duplicate of the card you are going to force

The Setup

Begin by selecting a card to force. Appearancewise, a face card will look best. Preset a duplicate card faceup under a white tablecloth. If the card is slightly visible through the cloth, position a cup or plate on top of it until you are ready to perform the trick.

The Stack

Force the card as normal. Hold up the top of the deck so your child sees his selection. Place the cards facedown on the table so that they land squarely on top of the hidden card. Add the rest of cards to the stack. The selected card now sits at the bottom of the stack directly on top of its duplicate, which sits beneath the tablecloth.

Take a spoon in your right hand as if it were a magic wand and tap the stack three times.

HIDDEN DUPLICATE CARD

The Sneak

Draw focus to your right hand by looking at it and lifting the spoon. As you dip the spoon into a glass of water, take the deck with your left hand, holding it facedown with your thumb on the bottom card.

While your child watches you scoop some water into the spoon, bring your left hand just below the table's edge and secretly drop the bottom card into your lap. As your right hand lifts a spoonful of water from the cup, your left hand casually sets the cards back on the table and off to the side.

The Stunner

Dump the spoonful of water dramatically onto the tablecloth above the hidden card. The tablecloth will become instantly transparent, bringing your child's card magically into view. As your child stares in wonder, secretly remove the duplicate from your lap, sneaking it into your shirt, your pants, or your sock.

Your Kid's an Ace

In this unique card trick, your kid ends up being the magician by magically dealing the four aces.

Begin with the four aces secretly on top of the deck. Hand the cards to your kid and ask her to deal the cards one at a time facedown into a single pile. After she deals about eight to ten cards, tell her she may stop dealing anytime she wants. When she stops, take the undealt cards from her hand and set them aside.

Have your child take her pile and deal four new ones adding one card at a time to each pile until all the cards are gone.

When she is finished dealing, have her turn over the top card of each pile. She will be surprised to discover that has dealt the four aces to the top of the pile.

22
Dad Goes Mental
The Amazing Dadini's Mind-Reading Madness

Imagine if you will, that you were able to read your kid's thoughts. The power would alter your perception of reality. It would provide you with unimaginable insight into the father/child relationship. Most importantly, it would let you do some pretty nifty tricks!
Try out these telepathic treats and see what your kid thinks!

Colorvision Crayon Caper

Display the full spectrum of your psychic abilities by identifying the color of five different crayons held completely out of your view.

Begin with both hands behind your back. Have your child give you five crayons so you cannot see them. Turn to face her, keeping the crayons behind you, and tell her you are going to use your Colorvision to name the color of each crayon without looking at any of them.

As you explain this, take the crayons into the palm of your left hand. Bring one of the crayons to your left fingertips and secretly mark your right thumbnail. Draw a small line across the face of the nail or scrape a bit of the crayon underneath.

Bring your empty right hand forward. Point to your daughter's palm, asking her to hold it out so you can return the crayons. As you do this, sneak a peak at your thumb, making sure you hold it at an angle where your child cannot see it. When you see the mark, you will know the color of the crayon you are holding in the fingertips behind your back. (Let's say it's red.)

Put your right hand behind you again and grab the red crayon. Pretending to search blindly, slide a second crayon into your left fingertips and mark your right thumbnail with a new color. When the nail is marked, say, "I will now hand you the red crayon!"

Bring your right hand forward and place the red crayon into your child's hand. As you do, sneak a peek at your thumbnail to determine the color of the next crayon ready to be grabbed. Repeat the process until all five crayons have been returned. Finish the routine by secretly wiping the evidence off your thumb.

DUH (Dad's Useful Hints): Pretending to have Colorvision will not work if you are actually color-blind.

The Precisely Calculated Surprise

WHAT YOU'LL NEED: A dictionary • An envelope • Pencil and paper

If your kid can handle a little addition and subtraction, astonish him with a seemingly impossible prediction.

The Prelude

Present your child with the family dictionary so he notices a sealed envelope sticking out as a bookmark. Open the book to the marked page to reveal the word *surprise* written on the outside of the envelope. Read him the definition of the word *surprise* from the same page. Close the book, place the envelope on top, and hand him a pencil.

The Math

1. Ask your child to write down a three-digit number in which all three digits are different.

2. Next, ask him to reverse the order of the digits.

3. Have him write both numbers down and subtract the lesser one from the greater one.

4. Ask your child to reverse the result of his subtraction, then add the two together.

5. Have him draw a vertical line between the third and fourth digit.

The Aftermath

Explain that the first three digits represent a page of the dictionary and that the last digit represents a word on that page. Have him turn to the proper page and count down the correct number of entries. Ask him to read the word aloud.

The Zinger

Tell him it's time for the surprise. Hand him the envelope and ask him to open it up. When he does, he will find a piece of paper with a single word written on it. Incredibly, the word will match the one he has just read aloud!

The Explanation

How does this surprising prediction work? Incredibly well, that's how!

We can't explain the exact mathematical formula, but we can assure you that the answer is always 1089! All you need to do is set things up ahead of time by finding the proper entry and sealing the word in the envelope marked *surprise!*

IMPORTANT NOTE: If the result of the subtraction is a two digit number, simply place a zero in front it. (**Example: 615 – 516 = *0*99.**)

The Psychic Sidekick

The family's coming over for dinner and they're expecting to be entertained. Give them the unexpected with a quick-paced comedy routine straight from the days of vaudeville. Turn your child into The Amazing Kidini and amaze your guests with your ESP (Extraordinary Silly Performance).

Performance Notes

The mind-reading gags in this routine can be mixed and matched in any order. Once you get the hang of them, you'll be able to create new ones of your own. Rehearse the routine with your kid until you can both perform rapidly.

Create an Amazing Kidini costume by making a cape from a bedsheet and a turban from a bath towel. Use a bandana as a blindfold. Gather the family into one room. Set a chair in the center of your "stage" and drape the blindfold over the back. Have your child wait in the next room wearing the costume.

DUH (Dad's Useful Hints): The more fun you have performing this, the more fun your audience will have watching it.

The Routine

DAD: Ladies and gentlemen, you are about to behold an unforgettable performer with unexplainable powers. A psychic wonder with talents of epic proportion. A soothsayer who has astonished the world . . .

KID: (Peeking in) Can you hurry it up, Dad? It's almost my bedtime.

DAD: Right! Please welcome my psychic sidekick. A small medium at large. . . . The Amazing Kidini!

(Kidini enters and sits. Dad puts the blindfold over Kidini's eyes.)

DAD: The Amazing Kidini is . . . All Knowing . . . All Seeing . . . All Hearing . . .

KID: What?

DAD: I said "All Hearing!"

KID: Oh.

KID: Let's show the audience your mental powers!

KID: I'm telepathic, Dad. You're mental!

DAD: Right. **(Dad moves into the audience.)** I am now going to hold up an object. As I do, The Amazing Kidini will use sightless vision to divine its identity, demonstrating mental prowess beyond human comprehension.

KID: Huh?

DAD: He will tell us what it is without looking!

KID: Right!

(Dad goes around the room borrowing objects from relatives.)

DAD: I am holding an object. Take your TIME. You'll get it in a SECOND.

KID: It's a watch!

DAD: Absolutely correct! This one should be easy to SEE. Think CLEARLY. Don't make a SPECTACLE of yourself.

KID: A pair of glasses!

DAD: Unbelievable! PICTURE this one in your mind. You should get it in a FLASH.

KID: A camera!

DAD: Astonishing! Will you kindly tell me what kind of coin I am holding?

KID: Round.

DAD: More specific.

KID: Very round.

DAD: Use your five senses!

KID: A nickel!

DAD: Amazing! I am holding an object that begins with the letter *F.*

KID: A Phone book!

DAD: No . . . an *F!*

KID: A photograph!

DAD: How does he do it?

DAD: What color is this lady's hair?

KID: Have her step forward.

DAD: Step forward, BLONDIE.

KID: She's a blonde!

DAD: He does it again! I have borrowed something from this man. Your first STEP is to tell me what it is. Don't make a HEEL of yourself.

KID: A shoe!

DAD: Yes! Tell us something about the owner of this shoe.

KID: He is going on a short journey.

DAD: (Throws the shoe across the room) Absolutely correct!

DAD: For our finale, I have chosen a number between one and one million.

KID: What's the number?

DAD: Three hundred and seven.

KID: Absolutely correct!

DAD: Ladies and gentlemen! The Amazing Kidini!

(Kidini stands and bows in the wrong direction. Dad removes Kidini's blindfold and the two bow together to thunderous applause.)

23
Moron Magic Show
Super-Stupid Sleight of Hand

Prove how silly you can be with insane illusions certain to drive
your kids crazy (or at least, make them think you're a nut!).

The Moron Magic Music

Create your own background music by singing the word *dad* over and over again. Choose a snappy melody (a show tune, circus music, sixteenth century Italian baroque opera), then speed it up and slow it down to punctuate your performance.

Make funny faces as you make your music and sing through the entire act unless otherwise instructed.

The Moron Magic Routine

Act One: Flying Fingers

Hold up the index finger of your left hand. Hold your right hand in a fist. Smash the two hands together so it appears that the finger has jumped from the left hand to the right. (**MORON MEMO:** If you can't figure out how to do this, you are already a moron and don't need this trick to prove it.)

The rest is up to you. Leap multiple fingers with a single smash. Hold up five fingers and jump them to another hand one at a time. Pretend to bite off your thumb then pull it out of your ear. Keep the fingers flowing until they have all returned to their proper places.

Act Two: Linking Rings

Convert your index fingers and thumbs into two solid and separate rings. (**MORON MEMO:** This is done by placing the tips together to form a circle. It does not involve stitching, welding, or glue products of any type.)

Tap the rings together to show that they cannot be linked. Place both hands behind your head, pause for dramatic effect, then bring them forward magically intertwined. Continue connecting and disconnecting behind your head, behind your back, and under your legs. For a fun finish, have the rings lock you in an awkward position so you have to contort to escape.

Act Three: Music Muffler

Point an index finger up and wave it playfully, then do the same with the other. Do a little dance, then bring the fingers into your ears. As soon as you do, stop your "dad" music, but keep your mouth moving like you are still singing at full volume. (**MORON MEMO:** No one has gone deaf. The gag is that your fingers in your ears have somehow muffled your kid's hearing.)

Remove both fingers and allow the music to resume instantly. Repeat the gag a number of ways, fingers in the opposite ears, one finger in one ear with your mouth shifted to sing from the other side.

Act Four: Wacky Water Glass

Display a clear glass of water in one hand and a dish towel in the other. Place the towel over the glass, then wave your free hand as if to make the water disappear. Turn your back, pull off the towel, chug (but don't swallow) the contents, replace the towel, and turn back. Resume waving your free hand, still singing your "dad" song (perhaps gargling it), then pull the towel away to reveal an empty glass.

Repeat the act, this time spitting the water back. Towel up some spilled beverage, reveal a (semi) full glass, and offer your kid a sip.

(**MORON MEMO**: The bigger the mess, the bigger the laughs, but the bigger the chances of trouble with Mom. We say, suffer for your art!)

Act Five: Vanishing Leg

Dangle a towel from your fingertips so it touches the floor. Lift the towel to reveal both your legs on the ground, then lower it again. Lift the towel bringing a leg along with it so it appears to vanish. (**MORON MEMO**: Do not panic. The leg is not gone. You are simply standing on one foot.)

Lower the towel (and the leg) then lift the towel to reveal the leg fully restored. Repeat the steps to make the opposite leg disappear.

For the grand finale, spread both legs wide, and lift the towel to reveal nothing below it. Finish your "dad" song with a flourish, then bow awkwardly from your wacky spread-leg position.

PART VI

The Amazing Dad as

The Greatest Showman on Earth

24

Leader of the Band
Looney Tunes for Loonier Instruments

The Amazing Dad may not have studied musical theory, but he has developed one: Play with an object long enough and it will play a tune. Perform a medley of musical feats, then teach them to the kids. A little creativity can be instrumental in turning your tike into a master musician.

The Harmoni-Comb

Here's a homemade instrument that creates a truly stylish sound. Grab an ordinary comb and a sheet of wax paper. If you don't have any wax paper (or have no idea what it is or where it would be located), try some aluminum wrap, some plastic food wrap, or chewing gum wrappers.

Hold the paper against one side of the comb, and bring the other side up to your mouth. Press the teeth of the comb against your lips and make a *doot doot* sound. It works and sounds just like a kazoo, but it is easier to part with when you are finished!

The Nose Guitar

If you can't teach your kid to pick a guitar or a banjo, at least you can teach him to pick his nose. Point a finger and press it against the outside of your nose, flattening a nostril. Begin humming a long steady note. With your free hand, point a finger and gently tap or strum on the open nostril.

Changing rhythm or pitch can create a variety of sounds from a country twang to a Hawaiian ukulele. With proper humming and strumming, you have the opportunity to turn your nose into a melodious musical instrument. Don't blow it!

The Raisin Box Trumpet

Fold back the lid of a snack-sized raisin box and place your lips around the entire opening. A funny horn-noise will escape from the bottom when you blow.

DUH (Dad's Useful Hint): Empty the box first or the *raisins* will escape from the bottom when you blow.

The Grass Flute

BLADE OF GRASS

Find a tall, thick blade of grass. Bring the palms of your hands together (as if praying that this trick will work) holding the blade of grass between the thumb knuckles and the balls of the hand. Blow a gentle, steady stream of air through the opening created by the two thumbs and a whistle sound will emerge. Tell mom you are cultivating instruments for the Grass Flute Festival and see how long you can get away without mowing the yard.

The Straw Whistle

Hold a straw straight up and down in one hand. Blow straight across the top opening to produce a whistle. Slide your other hand up and down the straw, pinching it to change the pitch.

The Phoney Keyboard

The keys to a cool tune are right on your phone. Call home, punch the proper pattern, and produce incredible melodies.

DUH (Dad's Useful Hints): Beginning a song when you can hear a dial tone may produce incredible phone bills. Make sure the kids know this!

Here are three phone favorites:

"Mary Had A Little Lamb"
3212333 222 399 3212333322321

"Jingle Bells"
333 333 39123 666 6633 3332232 9
333 333 39123 666 6633 3399621

"Happy Birthday"
112163 112196 1108521 008121

25

Dancing Machine

Cutting up When Cutting a Rug

Dads are destined to be dance partners with their kids. Whether it's a party or a private practice, little eyes will some-day look up and ask you to lead the way. Here are some steps to help you face the music.

Tango

Wrap one arm around each other, extending and linking the other. Get cheek to cheek and walk forward with your hands extended. If your child is small enough, lift and carry her.

When you've gone as far as you can (you've left the dance floor, run into a wall, or collided with a dancer who refuses to budge), shout, "Turn!" Flip your faces, extend the opposite arms, and move in the new direction.

Two Step

Stand face-to-face, hold your child's hands, and lift his feet onto yours. Sway side to side or take steps around the room. Whether you make it stylish or silly, your child will have fun following your fancy footwork.

Hokey Pokey Hokiness

The Hokey Pokey is one of the world's easiest dances. The lyrics tell you exactly what to do. The next time you find yourself circling up, add some spice by slipping in some of these silly extras:

1. **Right Foot/Left Foot**—Put your feet in pretending to stomp on bugs.

2. **Right Hand/Left Hand**—Reach across the circle, smile and shake hands with some-one on the other side.

3. **Right Hip/Left Hip**—Wiggle wildly, giggling as much as possible.

4. **Right Elbow/Left Elbow**—Shake your elbows in a flapping motion. Cluck loudly like a chicken.

5. **Head**—Lean it in and shake it furiously like a heavy-metal headbanger.

6. **Backside**—Back in, shake your booty, giggle, and shout, "No peeking!"

7. **Whole Self**—Jump in joyfully, then lift a leg and grab a knee like someone has landed on your foot. Hobble your way through the end of the song.

AMAZING DAD MOMENT
Wedding Dancer

One of my favorite father-stories took place during a recent family wedding. When the band played a song that sent all the dancers to their seats, my husband took our five-year-old daughter's hand and led her to the empty dance floor.

Taking Wendy into his arms, he began moving from one side of the dance floor to the other. He lifted her high into the air, spun her so her feet flew to the side, and pulled her in close to dance cheek to cheek. Wendy's laughter (and my husband's showmanship) attracted the attention of the guests, especially the young ones.

Our twin nieces rushed to the dance floor and requested a dance. My husband smiled and used his foot to indicate where they should wait. He dipped my daughter for a big finish, then kissed her on the forehead as he set her down.

My husband lifted the twins into his arms and began a double spin, oblivious to the fact that other children were now heading for the dance floor. By the time he was setting the twins down, there were nearly a dozen children waiting in line for a dance. At the back of the line was Wendy, waiting patiently for a second turn.

Invent-a-Dance

Help your kid invent original dances by combining classic moves with crazy ones. Here are some hints to get you moving.

Animal Dance

Pick a critter and predict how it might dance. The Elephant? Swing an arm from your face like a trunk and stomp around the room. The Caterpillar? Squirm on the floor, roll into a cocoon, then blossom into a butterfly. Need ideas? Take a quick trip to the zoo, sing to a hippo, and see how he sways.

Appliance Dance

Choose a common item, then supply some steps. The Toaster? Stand side by side like slices of bread, squat, pause, and pop up. The Sprinkler? Rapidly pat the back of your head, stick out a hand like a sprayer, and turn in a circle. If you spark a new craze, your household dance could become a household name!

Around the World in Eighty Dances (or Fewer)

Different places have different dances, and you can try them all. Mix an Irish jig with a Hawaiian hula and a Chinese fan dance for a routine that takes you around the world.

Crazy Combo

Take two or more dances that have become tiresome (the bunny hop, the conga, the electric slide) and combine them into something special. Our favorite is the swimbo: the limbo while doing the swim.

Decade Dance

Turn the floor into a time machine by mixing dance crazes from multiple decades. Start with some swing dancing (forties) followed by the hand jive (fifties), the twist (sixties), the bump (seventies), some break dancing (eighties), and the macarena (nineties). Add your own move to represent the millennium.

Never-Took-a-Lesson Dance

Show off your natural talents by doing dances that others pay a fortune to learn. Tap dance your way through a jazz-influenced mambo or perform an interpretive square dancing ballet.

26
Clowning Around
Classic Bits and Slapstick Schtick

It has been said that laughter is the best medicine. It has also been said that a smile is contagious. Investigate this comical anomaly with some guaranteed giggle-getters. Look at life through a funny nose and glasses and see how happy you can make your kid—and yourself.

The Pratfall

The pratfall is a comedy standby. Your kids stand by. You fall down. Everyone cracks up. There are two simple steps:

1. Stand or walk normally.

2. Collapse to the floor.

Act like you are fainting, pretend to be slipping, or just drop for no apparent reason when your kids least expect it. Make the fall look foolish (flailing arms, silly scream) so your kids will know it's all in good fun.

DUH (Dad's Useful Hint): Fall safely. Your kids won't crack a smile if you crack your skull. (Then again, that might crack them up, too!)

The Double Take

The double take is a laugh-inducing look that kids love. Follow these steps:

1. Look at your child as if nothing special is going on.

2. Look away casually.

3. Look back quickly, wide-eyed, like you can't believe what you are seeing.

The key to a good double take is timing. Each step should be solid and separate, and your child should witness all three. To add a little flair, shake your head quickly before looking back at your child, include a little sound effect, and bug your eyes as wide as possible. Watch old comedies and cartoons for good examples (or just watch them for a good time!).

Silly Face

Facial features have formal functions, but they can also be flat-out funny. Mess your hair, cross your eyes, pull your ears, scrunch your nose, puff your cheeks, pucker your lips, and stick out your tongue, mugging in a mirror until you've found the perfect combination.

Sneak the face in while helping with homework, in the middle of a meal, even reflected in a rearview mirror. A well-placed silly face will create a smile every time.

Funny Exit

Leave your child laughing by strolling out of the room in a strange way. Start with these classic moves, then develop a wacky walk of your own.

The Charlie Chaplin—Bring your heels close together, point your toes out, and waddle with short, fast steps. (Make sure you move silently.)

The Groucho Marx—Bend your knees, tilt your body forward at a precise fifty-five degree angle, and take long, silly strides. (Cigar and mustache optional.)

The Marilyn Monroe—Walk as if wearing high heels, wiggle your hips, and blow kisses. (She looked great doing this. You will look goofy. We hope.)

The Peter Lorre—Bend your fingers, tilt your head, and limp along with one leg dragging behind. (Scrunch your face, too. We have a hunch your kid will laugh.)

The Neil Armstrong—One giant step for man. One giant leap for mankind. One giant way to add a little atmosphere to your exit.

POP TEN LIST
Ten Great Ways to Get a Giggle

1. **Pull out a Nutty Prop**—Funny nose and glasses, rubber chicken, squirting flower.

2. **Put on Some Crazy Clothes**—A tiny hat, a huge pair of pants, mom's high heels.

3. **Talk in a Goofy Voice**—A high falsetto, a low bellow, a bad impersonation.

4. **Tell a Funny Joke**—A tricky riddle, a daffy definition, a classic knock knock.

5. **Do an Impression**—Bacon frying, an alligator tap dancing, a blender gone berserk.

6. **Make an Odd Noise**—A squeaky door, a screeching monkey, a 1957 Studebaker with a bad muffler.

7. **Smash a Pie in Your Face**—Whip cream, shaving cream, Boston cream.

8. **Pretend to Get Hurt**—Stub a toe, smash a finger, bump your head.

9. **Answer the Phone in a Surprising Way**—*"Yellow!" "Joe's Pizza!" "Cookie Factory! Which crumb do you want?"*

10. **Call Your Kid a Silly Nickname**—Squinkywink, Princess Poutface, Mister Ridiculous.

27
Acting Up
Improvised Skits That Are Surefire Hits

Improvisations (or improvs) are silly scenes made up right on the spot. They foster creativity, teach teamwork, and tickle the funny bone.

Who/Where

Try cool jobs! Travel the world! Never leave the house! All you need are two paper bags, small scraps of paper, a marker, and a little imagination.

Write the word *who* on the first paper bag, then fill it with sheets of scrap paper each listing a cool job (ballet dancer, hot dog inspector, veterinarian for vampire bats).

Write the word *where* on the second bag, then fill it with scrap sheets naming interesting places to be (in a mall, on a raft headed over a waterfall, trapped in a giant box of buttered popcorn).

Randomly select a sheet from each bag, then combine the two to create a scene. You may become doughnut bakers in an African jungle or rodeo cowboys on the moon.

Act out the scene until it comes to a funny conclusion, choose two more papers, then begin a new scene. When you finish creating crazy scenes, store the bags so they can be used again.

Secret Sayings

Here's an improv that will put words in your mouth and a smile on your face.

Write a dozen silly sentences on scrap paper. Make up original sentences (*"Hand me a duck!" "My pet pancake lost her shoe.")* or use already famous lines (*"To be or not to be," "Marsha! Marsha! Marsha!"*).

Fold the papers, select two sentences each, and without peeking, place them in your pockets. Think of a cool place to be, then begin a scene. In the middle of the conversation, take a paper from your pocket and say exactly what is written there. This will send the story into a silly new direction. Go with it awhile, then have your child read one of her sentences the same way.

When you use up all four secret sentences, come to a conclusion, choose a new location, select four more sentences, and begin again. When done for the day, return all the papers to the bag, and store it safely to be used another time. Add new phrases and sentences whenever you choose.

Preposterous Props

Grab a paper bag and fill it with small items (a picture frame, a slotted spoon, a rubber frog). If you find lots of small things or a couple of cool big ones, fill two bags.

Choose a place to be and start a scene. Find a reason to reach into a bag ("Hey! Look what I found in my shoe!" or "I have the perfect cure for hiccups right here!"), then randomly remove an item. Whatever you choose must be used in the scene right away. Be creative. A dog bone could become a twirling baton. A paper cup could be turned into a tiny hat.

Work four props into the scene, come to a good ending, then begin anew. When done for the day, return the items to their proper places, or leave them in the bag so they may be used again. Just remember what's in there, in case Mom goes looking for that egg beater you used as a tickle machine to defeat the pirate with the coat-hanger hook.

Show Time: A Night at the Improv

Practice and perfect some improvs, then perform a few for family and friends. Invite guests, serve treats to get them in a good mood, and allow them to supply ideas. They can suggest jobs and places for a **Who/Where**, jot down sentences for **Secret Sayings**, and donate items of their own for **Preposterous Props**. After the show, take bows, thank the audience for their suggestions, and reward their efforts by signing a few autographs.

28

Half-Hidden Ha Ha's

Corniness Behind Counters, Couches, and Corners

The next time something comes between you and your child,
turn it into something special. Hide half of your body and
mime all sorts of madness.

Silly Smooch

Stand against the side of a doorway so your kids see you from behind.
Make loud kissing noises while running your hands up and down your
back like the hands of a sweetheart.

> **DUH (Dad's Useful Hints):** Keep the kiss rated G. You don't want
to embarrass the kids and have them walk out (or embarrass
yourself in case Mom walks in).

Knutty Knockout

Grab your kid's attention by having someone grab you.

Stand with the right side of your body hidden behind a wall. Bend your right
arm so the hand comes into view like a stranger is about to grab you. Bring
the right hand behind your head, get a grip on the left side, and pull. Give a
shriek as the top of your body falls out of sight, then go silent, leaving your feet sticking out
with your toes pointing up.

Sit up (your kid won't see you), press your palms on the floor, and slowly scoot yourself back. To your child, it will look like the stranger is dragging you away.

The Canoe

Begin behind one end of the couch with your knees slightly bent and your arms positioned as if gripping an oar. Paddle on the left, then on the right, walking swiftly forward with each stroke. Turn the boat around, pretend to spring a leak, and paddle to no avail. Toss water from the canoe, salute, and slowly sink from view.

The Elevator

Stand in the center behind the couch, press an imaginary button, bend your knees, and slowly sink from view. Raise up when desired, pausing halfway as if trapped between floors. Angrily press buttons, causing the elevator to move up, down, and even sideways at all sorts of silly speeds.

The Escalator

To ride down, stand on your toes behind one end of the couch, keep your back straight, and walk forward, slowly bending your knees. To ride up, begin in a squatting position, and walk the opposite way, slowly straightening your legs. Have the escalator shift speeds, bring you in the wrong direction, then stop and throw you off.

The Skateboard

Stand with knees slightly bent, but give the illusion that you are at your full height, then rise slightly as you mime stepping onto the board. Move smoothly and quickly, leaning left and right, bobbing up and down, and raising your arms as if balancing yourself. Mime quick turns, trick jumps, and a wipeout.

The Staircase

Begin on your tiptoes and walk forward, lowering yourself a little more with each step. To walk up, begin in a squat position, then slowly rise in the reverse direction. Eat a banana on the way down, tossing the peel behind you. Slip on it on the way back up, then tumble out of sight.

VARIATION: Create a spiral staircase by walking in circle. Drop an imaginary ball near the top, and chase it around and down.

29

A Tip of the Cap

Chapeau Stunts and Assorted Hat Tricks

The Amazing Dad is a man who wears many hats. All of them can be put to good use. Need a trick to amuse your kids? Use your head and use a hat!

Hand to Head

This stylish way of donning a cap is the perfect put-on.

1. Hold your arm straight in front of you with your palm up and a hat hanging from your fingertips. Make sure the hat is in the direction you want it to be on your head.

2. As you bend your elbow, bend your fingers so the top of the hat comes to rest on your wrist.

3. Bring your hand straight up and place the hat on your head.

If done in a fast and fluid motion, the hat appears to tumble across the arm and up onto the head. The kids will flip for it!

Foot to Head

You don't need incredible feet to perform this incredible feat, just a little determination. Put your best foot forward and place a hat on the tips of your toes. Fling your foot forward so that the hat flies up into the air, then position your head so the falling hat lands in its proper place.

Hat Toss

Remember the James Bond villain who threw his hat with deadly accuracy? You can do the same! You'll be delighting people, not destroying them, but it will still be a killer trick. Take a hat off your head, pretend it's a ring from a ring toss game, and fling it toward a target. Aim for a hat rack, a bedpost, or the back of a chair.

DUH (Dad's Useful Hints): Avoid expensive vases, combustible lamps, and any family-made pottery, no matter how unattractive.

Tricks for Two

To perform a hat trick in hockey, a player must score three goals. To perform a hat trick with your kids, a father should set three goals: Make it simple, make it silly, make it smooth. Try these on for size.

Hat Grab

Your kid wears the hat. He turns to walk away. You reach forward (palm down) and move it from his head to yours. You turn to walk away, he snatches it back the same way and places back on his head. Move the hat from head to head with no one wearing it for more than a few seconds at a time.

NOTE: Convert a Hat Grab into a Hat Pass by snatching your own caps and placing them directly on your partner's head.

Double Hat Grab

Add a second hat and stand face-to-face. Reach forward at the same time, grab each other's hats, then place them on your own heads. As soon as the hats are in position, grab again. Start slowly, develop a rhythm, then begin to speed it up. You may even choose to call out orders (Reach! Grab! Lift! Place!).

DUH (Dad's Useful Hints): For variety, try the Double Hat Pass. We haven't included instructions, but we're betting you'll figure out how to pull it off.

Hat Juggling

Tack a few hat tricks together and turn them into a juggling act. Choose hats that are sturdy and easy to handle, then combine a pattern of passes and grabs to get the hats bouncing back and forth between you. Work in any or all of the tricks you've learned and create some of your own (your child kicks the hat to your extended hand, you flip it on your head and she steals it).

Fill out your routine with silly jokes or perform silently to your favorite music. Rehearse until it flows smoothly, then show off your skills for friends and family. If it is good enough, they'll take their hats off to you.

PART VII

The Amazing Dad as

The MVP
(Most Valuable Pop)

30

Dad's a Sport

All-Star Athletic Antics

While showing your kids the finer aspects of sports, be sure to show off the funnier aspects as well. Surprise them with a silly stunt or trick shot and bring some joy back into the game.

Quarterback Sneak

Bring your throwing arm behind your head like a quarterback ready to pass a football. Use your free hand to wave and encourage your kid to "go long." As he turns to run, slip the ball into the back of your shirt (down through the neck or up through the bottom).

When he turns to you to look for the pass, follow through as if you have just thrown it. Lift your hand to your eyes as if watching the pass soar over his head and into the distance. When he turns away to look for the ball, remove it quickly from your shirt, then pretend to catch it as if it has just traveled all the way around the world.

Vanishing Pop Up

Use an underhand motion to toss yourself a pop fly. Start with the baseball below your waist and extend your arm straight above your head as you let the ball go. Repeat the move several times, gradually increasing the height. To vanish the pop fly, secretly snag the ball with your free hand on the way up, then marvel as if it has risen into the clouds. It gives a whole new meaning to the word *airball*!

Cool Pool Shot

WHAT YOU'LL NEED: Pool table • Quarter • Short, wide glass

Take a break from a game of billiards to perform a pool shot that the kids will flip for. Place a quarter on the side cushion so that it touches the edge but does not hang over. Put a short, wide glass on the wood behind it. Set the cue ball in the center of the table directly in front of the coin and glass. Strike the ball straight into the side to make the coin flip up and into the glass.

POP TEN LIST
Ten Basketball Shots to Try out and Teach the Kids

1. Alley Oop—Jump toward the hoop while your child throws the ball. Catch it in the air and lay it in. If you miss, call it an Alley Oops and try again.

2. Behind the Board—Looking at the back side of the backboard, toss the ball up and over and down into the hoop.

3. Big Bounce—Bounce the ball off the ground and into the basket. If the ball is not well inflated you're going to blow it.

4. Daddy Dunk—Lift your child so she can slam the ball. Turn her backward for a reverse dunk or spin her in a circle for a fantasy 360 jam. Let your kid lose her grip on reality, but make sure you don't lose your grip on your kid.

5. Granny Shot—Hold your arms straight down, then toss the ball under-handed.

6. Hook Shot—Turn your side toward the basket and hold the ball in the hand farthest away. Start at the waist, then shoot as if drawing a half circle. Let go of the ball as it reaches the top of your head.

7. Long Shot—Stand far away from the basket and throw baseball-style. Make sure you are far enough to make it look amazing, close enough to have a chance, and fit enough to retrieve it when you miss.

8. Over the Head—With your back to the basket, lean back and look at the hoop, then shoot over your head. (Try it without looking, too.)

9. Put back—If you miss a shot, jump for the rebound and shoot again before coming down. Repeat until you've made a shot (or a fool of yourself trying).

10. Whatever Shot—Create your own shot by combining ideas. How about a Back-to-the-Basket, Behind-the-Backboard, eyes-closed, volleyball Alley Oop?

31
Strokes of Genius
Cool Shots and Creative Courses

When you find your kids puttering around with golf, take a course of action and create a fairway of fun. Tee off on some of these great golf suggestions and you'll all have a swinging good time.

Stack 'Em up Pop-up Shot

WHAT YOU'LL NEED: Golf tee • Pitching wedge or nine iron • Two golf balls of same brand and condition

Push a golf tee into the ground until the top is perfectly level with the earth. Place a golf ball on top of the tee, then balance a second golf ball on top of the first. If the balls are the same brand and in good condition, this is easier than it sounds (and the kids will be impressed already!).

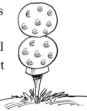

Take a pitching wedge or nine iron and hit the lower ball like a normal shot. The bottom ball will go forward, but the top one will shoot straight up into the air. Catch it in your hat for a flashy finish.

Pool Cue Putt

Next time you have a short putt (on the green or on the mini-golf course), lay flat on your stomach, turn the putter around, and use the handle like a pool cue. "Little, white ball. Forward pocket!"

AMAZING DAD MOMENT
The Home-Movie Hole-in-One

My fondest golf memory was the time my dad made an eight-millimeter movie of me hitting a hole in one. Dad planned the movie in four separate shots that we filmed back to back so there was no editing: the drive, the flight, the landing, and the roll into the hole.

Dad filmed the first three, but when it came to the fourth, we traded places. I did the filming so he could put the ball in the hole. He rolled it in perfectly on the first try.

After waiting a week for the film to be developed, this is what we saw: a nice close-up of me teeing off, a perfectly framed shot of the ball in flight, a beautiful panning shot of the ball bouncing onto the green, and a slightly unfocused, shaky shot of Dad rolling the ball right into the hole.

We laughed like crazy, and still do, every time we watch it.

Golf Coast

Bring an old putter and some regulation golf balls to the beach and build your own mini–golf course out of sand. Create tunnels, ramps, barriers, water hazards, and the ever-present sand trap.

Here are a few fun designs to get you started.

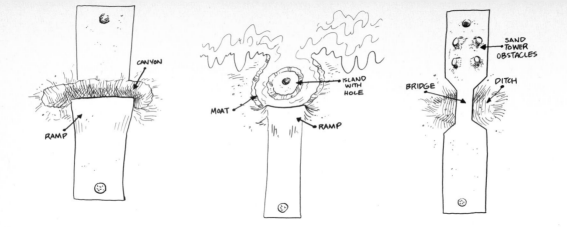

Putt Putt Palace

Convert your home into an indoor country club by designing holes for different rooms. Turn books into tunnels, blocks into ramps, and potted plants into unexpected hazards. Finish by putting into strategically placed plastic cups.

DUH (Dad's Useful Hints): Keep things safe by having the kids use plastic equipment. If things get a little messy, just consider it par for the course. Here are the blueprints for three challenging holes.

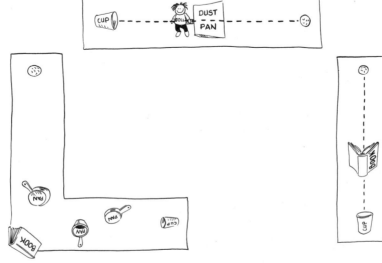

32

Making a Splash
Whimsical Water Play

**More than three-fourths of the world is covered in water.
You better get into it! Dip into your bag of tricks and cool
things off with these sensational water stunts. Just be sure to
put safety first!**

Dolphin Ride

Let your child lie flat against your back with her arms wrapped around your neck. Swim with "porpoise" through the water, splashing over and under the surface while your child hangs on happily.

Rocket Launch

Here's one that lets you and your kid have a real blast. Bend your knees slightly, place your elbows against your waist, and hold your palms upward. Have your child sit on your open hands with his feet on your knees. Thrust your child into the air by straightening your legs and extending your arms in one swift motion. Stand by to help with recovery after splashdown.

DUH (Dad's Useful Hints): You do not have to wait a half an hour to swim after launch.

Magic Massage

Get your child to float on his back, relaxing and remaining still. Submerge, then rise slowly until you are inches below your child's back. Wave your hands to create tiny caressing currents near your child's head and feet, then blow bubbles directly on his back. Keep your hands moving as you pop up for breath, and the massage can last as long as you like. When you are worn out, try to convince your kid to return the favor and create a Magic Massage for you.

Wave Maker

Standing in the shallow end, position a raft sideways in front of you and begin pushing it up and down on the surface. Your child may help push your raft, push on one of her own, or hold on to a wall and watch. When the waves really get rolling, place her onto the raft for a wild ride.

DUH (Dad's Useful Hints): You may not need to do this at the ocean.

Little Squirt

Fold your fingers so they lie flat against your lower palm. Lay your thumb on top, leaving a little hole in the center of the fist. Lower your hand into the water, leave your thumb slightly above the surface, and let a little water slip into the hole. Squeeze your fingers into your palms and send the water squirting up into the air.

Floating Fountain

Try this if you've mastered the little squirt. It is sure to muster big smiles. Fill your mouth with water when no one is looking. It's part of the surprise, and you don't want to be caught drinking from the pool, anyway. Slip into a floating position. Extend your arms with both hands in the Little Squirt position. Squeeze your palms to create two tiny waterspouts. Wait until you have your child's attention, then send a stream of water straight up from your lips. You may get drenched, but you'll soak up the applause.

POP TEN LIST
Ten Cool Ways to Make a Splashy Entrance

1. The Cannonball—Jump into the air, making yourself as round as possible by wrapping your arms around your bent knees.

2. The Cartoon Cliff-Fall—Take a leaping step, realize you've left the ground, then run in the air as you fall.

3. The Distracted Drop—Read an imaginary newspaper, or glance at your watch as you unknowingly walk off the edge.

4. The Flip—Forward or backward then downward.

5. The Flop—Stand tall, hands pointed above your head as if ready to dive. Fall straight forward into the water.

6. The Flying Flop—Leap flat out over the water, spread your arms and legs, and fall belly first.

7. The Jackknife—Jump into the air, wrap both arms around a bent knee. Extend the other leg straight down toward the water.

8. The Plunge—Turn away from the pool, spread your arms, and fall straight back.

9. The Sleeper—Leap up, fall sideways, and put your hands on the back of your head as if resting.

10. The Slipper—Pretend to step on a banana peel and tumble in.

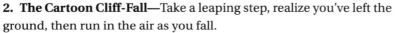

33

Wrestlemaniac

Safe and Silly Skirmishes

If your kid loves to play-fight, join in and play along (just remember to play fair). Here are three rules of engagement that guarantee a good time: 1. Emphasize the play, not the fight. 2. Don't underestimate your own strength. 3. Let your child win (most of the time).

Tricky Tickle Fight

Cross your arms, setting an elbow on top of an elbow crease. Bring your lower hand up, spread your fingers, and place it over your face as a protective mask. Peek through your fingers and try to tickle your child. Have your child set up the same way, fending off your tickles as she tries to tickle you.

Thumb Wars

Bend your fingers toward your palm, hook hands with your son, and set your thumbs side by side. Bounce the thumbs up and down and recite the following poem: "One, two, three, four. I declare a thumb war." Then try to pin each other's thumbs flat. Here are a few tricks to try or to teach:

The Delay: Hold your thumb up waiting for your kid to grow impatient. As soon as he makes a move, drop your thumb on his.

The Trap: Lay your thumb flat, wait for your kid to try to pin it, then dodge and trap his.

The Tickle: Lean your thumb forward so that it tickles your child's thumb while it is still in the air. When your son tries to sidestep the tickle attack, push his thumb in the same direction for a pin.

Balloon Fencing

Inflate long, thin balloons and take a stab at fencing. Hold the end of a balloon, fold your free hand behind your back, stand face-to-face, then wiggle the balloons to work your way into scoring position. Pressing the tip of your balloon against an opponent's belly earns you five points; twenty-five points ends the match.

SAFETY NOTE: Uninflated balloons or popped fragments are choking hazards for children and animals.

Staring or Smile Contest

Stand slightly apart, lock eyes, and see who can go longest without blinking. Make the contest longer and sillier by making faces until somebody smiles.

Grass Battle

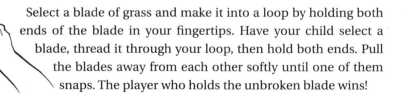

Select a blade of grass and make it into a loop by holding both ends of the blade in your fingertips. Have your child select a blade, thread it through your loop, then hold both ends. Pull the blades away from each other softly until one of them snaps. The player who holds the unbroken blade wins!

Pillow Fight

Find a safe area to spar, then playfully push pillows against your kid. Let him pound you with all his might while you pretend to struggle against his super strength. Teach him some tricky pillow maneuvers, then fall for them over and over again.

POP TEN LIST
Ten Pillow Fighting Maneuvers to Teach Your Kid

1. The Ol' Switcheroo—She holds a pillow in her right hand, waves it flamboyantly, then sneaks in a quick shot with a pillow held in her left.

2. The Cymbal Crash—He takes pillows into both his hands, gets your head in between, then brings the pillows together.

3. The Bumper Car—She holds a pillow in front of her body and bumps into yours.

4. The Sled—He holds a pillow in front of his body, then jumps, pillow first, on top of you.

5. The 360—She swings and misses, spins around, and gets you on the way back.

6. The Drop and Chop—You swing down, miss, and fall to the floor. He bonks you on the back of your head.

7. The Smack Backward—She turns her back to you, grabs a pillow with both hands, and hits you by swinging straight back over her head.

8. Bombs Away—He tosses a pillow up high so it clunks you from above.

9. Look Behind You!—She says the words, then whacks you when you look.

10. Down and Dirty—He says his pillow has a spot on it, then pushes it into your face when you bend over to look.

AMAZING DAD MOMENT
Pillow Fight Phrases

My son and I have a series of magic pillow fighting phrases that he can shout out to alter the course of events.

"Release!" causes all pillows to instantly drop from my hands.

"Slow Motion!" sends me into a turtle's pace so he can outrun me to a loose pillow.

"Open Sesame!" instantly removes him from a sheet or blanket I have tossed over his head.

"Switchback!" reverses our positions. If I have him playfully pinned beneath a pillow, the phrase spins us 180 degrees so that he is pinning me.

"Freeze!" turns me into a statue so he can escape an offensive attack and pummel me senseless. (For some reason, that is his favorite!)

PART VIII

The Amazing Dad as

The Maître d' of Mayhem

34
Dinner Music
Terrific Tunes at the Table

Kids get a bang out of drumming on pots and pans, but there are classier (and quieter) ways to cook up music. Your kitchen cabinets can open the door to a wide variety of symphonic possibilities.

Glass-ical Music

If your child is thirsting for a new way to make music, here's a surefire trick to quench the desire. Find three to seven glasses. They don't have to be identical. They don't even have to be clean. They just have to be glass. Fill each one with a different level of water; the one on the far left should be filled almost to the top, with each subsequent glass being filled a little less. The set can now be played like a xylophone.

Take a spoon, hold it loosely, and tap the side of each glass. A gentle tap will produce a lovely tone. (A forceful tap will shatter the mood and produce nothing more than a mess.)

Begin by playing a simple scale (starting left on glass number one and moving right to glass number seven), then progress to some easily recognized tunes. Here's a first-class six-glass song to get you started.

"Twinkle Twinkle Little Star"

1	1	5	5	6	6	5	4	4	3	3	2	2	1
5	5	4	4	3	3	2	5	5	4	4	3	3	2
1	1	5	5	6	6	5	4	4	3	3	2	2	1

A MUSICAL NOTE: To make the music a bit more beautiful, secretly add a different-colored drop of food coloring to each glass before pouring water in from a pitcher.

Glass Harp

If there are crystal glasses on the table, you've got a beautiful instrument right at your fingertips. Pour any amount of water into a crystal glass, then wet the upper part of your index finger. Begin rubbing your finger around the surface of the rim at a steady pace and it will magically emit a soft tone.

Fill a few glasses at varying heights, then try to create a little melody. (The higher the water level, the higher the tone.) Entertain the kids with an improvised selection, or secretly rehearse to produce a recognizable tune.

Dinner Bells

Although this trick looks silly at the start, it has a sensationally symphonic finish. Knot a spoon at the center of a long piece of string or yarn. Wrap the ends of the string around each of your child's index fingers, then place the tips of the index fingers into his ears.

Have your child swing the spoon so it strikes the edge of a table or a chair. When he does, he will hear a beautiful sound like the distant chimes of a church bell.

The next time you ask him if he'd like to try the trick, you are sure to get a ringing endorsement.

Rhythmic Spoons

Here's the scoop on a classic right from hillbilly country. Grip two spoons tightly in one fist. Turn the spoons back-to-back. Hold the top spoon between your thumb and your index finger. Hold the bottom spoon between your index finger and your middle finger. Keep the backs of the spoons a half inch apart so they will click together when you hit them against something.

Sit (or stand with a leg on a stool), then put your free hand palm down a few inches above your leg. Start a rhythm by hitting the spoons down on your leg, then up against your palm, going back and forth between the two. Create multiple clicks by spreading the fingers of your free hand and sliding the spoons up and down against them. Keep things interesting by mixing in an occasional smack against your stomach, your arms, or your feet.

35
Hi Ho Silver

Hanging Spoons, Floating Forks, and Cutting up with Cutlery

Not since the dish ran away with the spoon (and took the fork in the road) has there been such silliness with silverware. Take a stab at these stunts and your cup will runneth over with fun.

Spoon on Your Nose

Secretly breathe hotly on the bowl of a spoon. (This is not something you want to be seen doing openly.) Hang the bowl from the tip of your nose and converse casually as it dangles there.

DUH! (Dad's Useful Hints): Stick with spoons so you don't get stuck. Attempting a Fork on the Nose can lead to the visually stunning, yet horrendously painful, Fork in the Eye.

Floating Fork

Your child sees this.   He thinks this.   You do this.   Because of this!

A Well-Balanced Meal

WHAT YOU'LL NEED: A spooon • A fork • A toothpick • A glass

Try this clever silverware stunt and you'll be poised for success. Push the tip of a spoon into the tines of a fork. The two inner tines should clip on to the bowl of the spoon, the two outer tines on to the back. Stick one end of a toothpick between the middle two tines. Place the other side of the toothpick on the edge of a glass. With a little adjusting, the whole thing will balance perfectly.

AMAZING DAD MOMENT
A Sharp-Looking Stunt

For years I have amused my family with a silly, knife-sharpening gag. Sitting across from the kids at the dinner table, I pretend that my butter knife is too dull. I then place a clean plate between my knees and turn it into a sharpening wheel.

First I slide my fingers over the rim as if spinning the "wheel" toward me. I then bounce my legs steadily to keep it moving. Finally, I lower the butter knife to the plate and act like the friction from the "spinning wheel" is altering the blade. Since my kids see only the top half of the plate, it really looks like I am sharpening the knife. I have a lot of fun with it, too, examining the blade, mopping my brow, and whistling while I work.

To finish the act, I set the knife aside and stop the "spinning wheel" by dramatically grabbing it with one hand. To test my newly sharpened knife, I remove an imaginary hair, drop it on the blade, and pretend to see it being severed in two. I have taught my oldest son how to do the trick, and we have performed it together several times. My ultimate goal is to perform this "cutting edge" comedy routine with all three of my sons, simultaneously, side by side, at a family Thanksgiving feast.

36
Extraordinary Straws

Being Hip While You Sip

There are three things you don't want to do with straws: 1. Draw the short one in a difficult situation. 2. Try to build a wolf-proof home (especially if you're a pig). 3. Place one on a fully loaded camel's back. Anything else goes. Especially if the straws are the drinking kind.

Flying Wrapper

Rip off one third of a wrapper from a straw. Blow into the exposed side of the straw and send the remains of the wrapper flying. Teach your kids to aim for the trash can, but be prepared to become their favorite target.

Wrapper Worm

How do you make a straw wrapper come to life? Just add water. Scrunch a wrapper as tightly as you can down to one end, then remove it and place it on the table. Drip a single drop onto the wrapper, then watch it expand, inch forward, and worm its way into your child's heart.

Wrapper from the Ear

Secretly flatten a straw wrapper so it is long and thin. Zigzag fold it like an accordion, then close it into a little square. Pretend to scratch an itch, wedge one end into the opening of your ear, then get your kid's attention. Pull the loose end outward in a quick motion, and give a gasp or grunt as the long wrapper emerges.

Note: If your ear is too big to wedge the wrapper in tightly, pull it from your nose. If your nose is too big, your facial features are entertaining enough without the straws.

Straw Karate

Hold the ends of a straw with the thumb and index finger of both hands, then rotate your hands over each other slowly. The straw will roll tightly around both index fingers leaving a small section filled with pressured air in the center.

Lift your hands toward your child and ask her to bend a middle finger back and flick the middle section of the straw. If she strikes the section solidly, there will be a loud pop, and the straw will snap cleanly in half. Save both sides as a souvenir for your newly trained karate champion.

Backward Straw

Unwrap a straw, stick it into your glass, and blow bubbles. Act surprised, lift the straw, look at it, and say, "Oops. Must have put it in backwards!" Turn the straw around, insert the opposite end into the cup, and drink normally.

Spitballs

We're not going to cover this one, but we wanted you to know we thought about it. We're not just trying to dodge a sticky subject. There's just no need for a father to teach the fine art of spitballs to a child.

Some sneaky, so-called friend will corrupt your kid sometime between the second and fifth grade. Official certification will come in the form of a letter or phone call from a disgruntled teacher.

When you have the stern talk that inevitably follows, add a poetic touch by tossing in the phrase, "This is the last straw!" Your talk may keep your kid out of a wad of trouble, but he will no doubt pass the unsavory act on to someone else.

AMAZING DAD MOMENT
The Beverage Baffler

When my son ordered an orange soda at a fast-food place, I ordered a Sprite, placed lids on both drinks, and decided to play a trick.

As I grabbed the straws, I stuck one all the way into his orange drink. I secretly placed my finger over the top, lifted it up, then placed it into my cup, keeping my finger over the top until it touched the bottom. I now had a strawful of his drink hidden in my cup of Sprite.

I put a plain straw in his drink and gave it to him as I sat down. As he started sipping, I pretended to drink mine. I made a face, put my finger over the straw, and lifted it out. I let it spill onto a nearby napkin so it looked like I had been given an orange soda, too.

As Josh laughed, I pushed the straw back in and told him I would just have to get the color out. I slurped loudly, then popped the top off to reveal the orange color completely gone. Josh spent the rest of lunch sipping with a scrunched up face, trying to uncolor his drink.

37

Napkin Nonsense

A Puppet, a Play, and a Couple of Puzzlers

**Looking for a tidy trick or a neat stunt to amuse the kids?
Wipe the frowns off their faces and lap up the laughs with a
little hanky-panky.**

Cloth Napkin Duck

Create this friendly creature from a cloth napkin, and it's sure to quack up your kid. Form the head and beak by tying a knot in a corner. Hold the knot between the knuckles of your index and middle fingers. Create the body by wrapping the napkin around the fingers, then tucking it in the back. Fluff up the end to look like tail feathers, then place the tips of the index and middle fingers on the table as legs.

Waddle your duck around the table, sip up a small drop of water, or lay a hard boiled egg (gripped secretly in the fingers hidden beneath the napkin body).

Paper Napkin Play

Dads should never encourage kids to act up at the dinner table, but we can encourage them to act out. Use a single napkin to perform an original play and create a little after-dinner theatre.

Fold a napkin (paper or cloth) so it looks like a bow. Hold it on the top of your head as a bow for the heroine. Hold it under your nose as a mustache for the villain. Hold it under your chin as the bow tie for the hero. Move the napkin from place to place, changing your voice for each character and improvising the plot and dialogue.

Encourage the kids to rehearse their own scenes and after the next meal, allow them to entertain you.

Need story ideas? Have the hero and heroine out on a date with an evil waiter trying to sabotage their evening. Have the villain tie the hero to a railroad track so the heroine can come to the rescue. Have the villain demand rent from the heroine, only to be foiled by a millionaire neighbor. *Here's the classic routine:*

"You must pay the rent!"

"But I can't pay the rent!"

"You must pay the rent!"

"But I can't pay the rent!"

"I'll pay the rent for you!"

"My hero!"

"Curses! Foiled again!"

Cloth Napkin Knot

Twist a cloth napkin so it looks like a rope, then lay it down on the table. Challenge your child to grab both ends of the napkin and tie a knot in the center without letting go of either side (or tying it around her wrist).

When she tries and fails, set the napkin in front of you and surprise her with the simple solution. Cross your arms (basically tying them into a knot), then lower them to the napkin. Grab the left end of the napkin with your right hand and the right end of the napkin with your left hand. Without letting go, unfold your arms slowly and the knot will tie itself.

Torn and Restored Napkin

This trick involves two paper napkins (although you will make believe there is only one.) We've labeled them A and B for instructional purposes

DUH: (Dad's Useful Hints): Do not label them when you perform.

When your kid isn't looking, fold napkin A into a small square and hide it behind three closed fingers. Get your kid's attention, lift up napkin B, keeping A hidden behind it so your child doesn't know it is there.

Tear B into strips, then fold them into a square that is roughly the same size as A. As you do this, secretly reverse the napkins so the folded A is facing your child and the ripped B is facing you.

Slowly begin unfolding A. As the napkin opens and blocks your child's view, crumble B into a ball and hide it under your fingers. As you hand A to your kid to examine, secretly slip B into your pocket or drop it under the table.

Dad's on a Roll

Baffling the Kids with Bread

If there's a basketful of bread on the table, don't waste any dough. Make yourself a roll model and serve up a fresh batch of bread-winning stunts. It's the yeast that you can do.

Rubbery Roll

This surprising stunt makes it look and sound as if you are bouncing a roll off the floor and back up into the air. You'll have a ball performing it.

Sit down at a table across from your kid. Take a bite of a roll, mumble a comment like, "This is so chewy, it tastes like rubber," then thrust your arm down as if you are throwing it to the floor.

When your hand is below table level and hidden from your child's view, toss the roll right back up into the air. Keep your elbow straight and toss with your wrist only. If you keep the tossing motion out of view and stomp your foot to make a bouncing sound, it will look unbelievably believable.

Floating Roll

WHAT YOU'LL NEED: Roll • Napkin • Fork

You want to know how to make a roll appear to float? Stick a fork in it! Secretly place the fork into the side of the roll, then grip the handle between your thumb and index finger.

Hold a cloth napkin in both hands as if it were a tiny curtain, three fingers from each hand in front, the thumbs and index fingers behind. Keep the fork hidden along the top of the napkin and guide it so the roll appears to float up and peek over the top. Redirect the roll so it floats back under and into the center of the napkin. Let it dart left and right with its shape clearly visible beneath the cloth.

Coin in a Roll

WHAT YOU'LL NEED: Roll • Coin • Fork

This trick allows you to "roll" a coin by making it appear in the middle of bread that you have just broken open. Begin by giving your child a quarter and asking her to scratch an identifying mark onto it with a fork.

When she is finished, take the quarter with your left hand. Grab the coin with your right hand, then open it to show that the coin has vanished. *(See Chapter 20: Presto Change-Oh for the classic coin vanish.)*

Pick up a roll, placing it into your left hand directly on top of the coin which is hidden there. Dig both of your thumbs into the top of the roll and begin tearing it open. As you do, push the quarter up through the bottom so it is waiting for you in the center. Let your daughter remove the quarter to verify her markings while you finish tearing the roll in half and begin eating the evidence.

Blow Dart Dazzler

WHAT YOU'LL NEED: A toothpick • A straw • A roll

This is a sharp trick to perform for older kids. You are ***not*** really going to shoot a blow dart. Your child needs to understand this. If your kid is old enough to know that this is a trick that he shouldn't repeat, take your best shot at it.

Get your kid's attention, pick up a toothpick, and slip it into a straw. Bring the straw to your mouth so the toothpick rests near your lips ready to be blown out like a dart.

Grab a dinner roll and toss it into the air above you. Blow hard on the straw, then catch the roll as it falls. Lean over and show your kid that the toothpick is now stuck neatly in the side of the roll.

How did you do it?

You stuck a matching toothpick into the roll ahead of time, then held and tossed the roll so your kid couldn't see it. You squeezed down on the straw as you blew, then secretly dumped your toothpick in your lap as you leaned over to show off your striking success.

DUH (Dad's Useful Hints): Practice this one ahead of time so you don't end up swallowing the toothpick or shooting it across the room.

Go Nuts with Fruit

Producing Laughs with Produce

It may not be proper to play with your food, but sometimes the temptation is just too much to bear. If you're looking for something to make the kids smile, Mother Nature has provided a lot to pick from. Fruits are ripe with comedic possibilities and nuts can simply crack them up.

Presliced Banana

WHAT YOU'LL NEED: Banana • Hat pin or long needle

Have you heard of the new bananas being grown just for people who plan to put them in cereal? Well, neither has your kid. Introduce him to the appealing concept with a little preslicing monkey business.

Get a needle or a hat pin that is wider than the banana. Stick the pin into the peel someplace near the top. Wiggle it left and right slicing the fruit without disturbing the far side of the peel. Pull the pin out, move it a little lower, and repeat the process several times.

Begin breakfast with a tale of genetic engineering (these days, who doesn't?), then pass the banana to your kid to peel for himself. He'll be delighted to discover the pieces perfectly sliced for his bowl.

Nutty Sneeze Gag

Secretly conceal a cashew in your hand, then cover your nose as if you are about to sneeze. After a big buildup, sneeze with a mighty,

147

"Cashew!" letting it drop to the table. Say, "This cold is driving me nuts!" Pick up the cashew and pop it into your mouth.

Orange Peel Teeth

Cut an orange into quarters, then peel off one of the quarter skins. Take scissors and make an incision through the center of the skin leaving about a half inch on each end. Create teeth by making smaller cuts from the center incision straight up and down or diagonally.

Slip the peel under your lips and run your tongue along the backside to make the teeth wiggle. Wear the teeth orange-side out for hillbillies with badly brushed bicuspids or white-side out for monsters with funny, fuzzy fangs.

Peanut Gallery

Squeeze the upper half of a peanut shell and a tiny gap will open at the top. Let the gap close and pinch your earlobe so the entire peanut hangs like a dangling earring. Add an earring to the other ear then continue hanging peanuts on any part of your face you choose. Clip them to your chin, your eyebrows, and your nose until you look like a complete nut.

The Great Grape Routine

In this trick, two grapes are passed off as one, and one grape is passed through your head.

Secretly hide grape #1 in your ear, then get your kid's attention. Pop grape #2 in your mouth and pretend to swallow it whole. Bang the side of your head so grape #1 pops out. Pick grape #1 up with your right hand, grab at it with the left, but do a French Drop so it secretly remains in the right. (*See Chapter 20: Presto Change-Oh!*)

Take your empty left hand and pretend to smash grape #1 through the top of your head. Push grape #2 with your tongue so it peeks out of your mouth. Pull it back in and swallow it (really!). Lift your right hand, which your child thinks is empty, remove grape #1 from your child's ear, and swallow it (the grape, not the ear!).

Walnut Surprise

WHAT YOU'LL NEED: A walnut • Glue • Small object

Show your kid that things aren't always what they're cracked up to be.

Separate a walnut into two perfect halves, then clean out the inside. Fill the empty space with a silly object, then glue it back together.

Replace the nut with candy ("I've heard of candy with nuts in them, but never nuts with candy in them!"), money ("Wow! I guess it really does grow on trees!"), or a folded note (An "I got here first!" message from a squirrel).

Watermelon Pit Spittin' Spot

WHAT YOU'LL NEED: Watermelon (with seeds) • Muffin pan

Place a muffin pan on the ground. Assign point values to each section. Stand back a few paces, spit the pits, and see who earns the most points.

DUH (Dad's Useful Hints): This is an outside activity! Pit spittin' in the kitchen is forbidden.

PART IX

The Amazing Dad as

Mr. Mystery

Creature Features

Comical Character Creations

These crazy creatures are formed from one body or a combination of two. Join your talents with those of your kids and create monster fun!

Little Big Mouth

WHAT YOU'LL NEED: Blanket • T-shirt • Washable marker

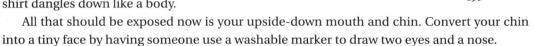

Here's a little lunacy that's sure to make a big impression. Lie on your back and dangle your head upside down off the back of the bed. Cover your body with a blanket and cover your eyes and nose with a loose T-shirt. Pull the neck up past your eyes and over your nose so the rest of the shirt dangles down like a body.

All that should be exposed now is your upside-down mouth and chin. Convert your chin into a tiny face by having someone use a washable marker to draw two eyes and a nose.

Your Little Big Mouth can now perform a short routine, tell a silly story, or lip-synch to a favorite song.

DUH (Dad's Useful Hint): If you draw the face yourself, do it before you turn upside-down and cover your eyes.

If your child would like to take part, turn her into a Little, Little Big Mouth. Audiences will flip for your funny act, and you're sure to receive quite a rush from performing it!

Tiny Tot

WHAT YOU'LL NEED: A pair of boots • A jacket or unbuttoned shirt

Have your daughter stand behind a table with her arms straight down into a pair of boots on the table. Turn a jacket or unbuttoned shirt backward and drape it over her shoulders.

Stand behind her, duck your head down, and extend your arms through the sleeves so your hands appear to be hers. You now have a tiny tot atop a table. You control the arms. She controls the legs. You both create comedy together.

Place a variety of items on the table (combs, toys, food) and let her play pretend. If she says, "I think I'll have a snack," you'll have to try to open the bag of cookies and feed her.

Daddy Long Legs

The setup for this one is simple, but the illusion is extraordinary. Lie on your back, either on the floor or on a bed, and cover your waist and head with a sheet. Have your son face your feet, sit on your stomach, and straddle your body. When he finds a natural kneeling position, comfortable for him, as well as for you, cover his legs with your sheet. From the front view, his little body looks like it has your long legs, especially if you wear similar-colored pants. You'll both get a kick out of it.

Mr. Shorty

Become a short guy in a short time with this easy guise. Place a pair of shoes on the ground, then kneel with your knees down on the openings meant for your feet. Turn toward your child with the lower half of your legs hidden behind you or under a blanket, and it will look like you have tiny legs wedged right into the shoes.

Play or perform for a while, then kneel your kid into a pair of shoes to create a Shorty Junior or Junior Miss. You can share some "little" moments that will produce very big fun.

Once you've played long enough (perhaps practicing in front of a mirror), create a comedy routine to perform for family and friends.

Creature Feature Archives

Make sure you get someone to take photographs or video so you can immortalize your creatures and send images to your family and friends.

41

The Haunted Hand

An Offhanded and Disarming Feat

As The Amazing Dad, you always have something up your sleeve. (Even when there's nothing there!) Try your hand at this gripping off-the-cuff routine and you'll be sure to hold your kid's attention.

How to Create the Haunted Hand

Put your right arm through the right sleeve of a loose-fitting jacket, then zip the jacket shut. Place the empty left sleeve into the left jacket pocket, fluffing it out like your arm is still there. Place your right hand in the right coat pocket. Place your left arm flat against your chest with the elbow at your belt and the Haunted Hand hovering just under the jacket collar.

What to Do with the Haunted Hand

Get near your child and act casually. Keep your right hand in your pocket whenever possible. Allow the Haunted Hand to slide out subtly and accomplish a simple task.

Have the Haunted Hand rise up and . . .

- adjust your reading glasses.

- hold a tissue so you can blow your nose.

- place a piece of candy in your mouth.

- scratch an itch on the side of your face.

- steal a piece of food you are about to eat.

- stir a cup you are holding near your mouth.

- wave to your child before vanishing.

- wipe your face with a handkerchief.

Do not draw attention to the Haunted Hand. Don't even notice it. Act as if everything is normal. When you are sure it has grabbed your kid's attention, launch into the Haunted Hand routine.

The Haunted Hand Routine

1. Make the Haunted Hand sneak out, tap you on a shoulder, then slip down as you look to see what tapped you.

2. Let the Haunted Hand sneak out, tap you on the other shoulder, then slip down again, just as you look.

3. Have the Haunted Hand repeat both moves, causing you to become increasingly frustrated.

4. Grow suspicious of your jacket. Take your good hand, pull the collar away from your neck, and peer inside.

5. Look up, smile toward your child, and give a "There's nothing in there" shrug.

> Pause to build suspense. . . .
>
> > Keep pausing . . . .
> >
> > > You want to make this good. . . .
> > >
> > > > Okay . . . now!

6. Have the Haunted Hand leap up from your collar and hover in front of your face. React with a silly look of surprise.

7. Move the Haunted Hand so it jumps forward with its fingers spread and palms your face like a basketball.

8. Grab the Haunted Hand by the wrist (with your good hand) and try to pry it loose. Kick your legs crazily, twist and turn, and let the battle rage as long as you'd like.

9. Let the Haunted Hand break free from your face and slip back into the collar. Run it right down through the empty sleeve so it can emerge from your pocket as if it were there the entire time.

10. Use both good hands to quickly remove the jacket and toss it to the side.

11. Kick at the jacket as if checking to see if the Haunted Hand is still there.

12. Give a sigh of relief as you discover it has vanished, then give a gasp of dismay as you realize it has simply escaped to return another day!

DUH (Dad's Useful Hints): Remove jewelry before performing. Watches and rings worn by the Haunted Hand should not suddenly show up on *yours*.

42
Phenomenal Photographs

Perplexing Pictures of the Paranormal

Why are kids fascinated by unexplained phenomena? It's an unsolved mystery. If stories of monsters and saucers bring sparkles to their eyes, imagine what photos can do!

Little Creatures

Get two kids, then choose a mythical creature small enough for one of them to hold in the palm of her hand (a leprechaun, a fairy, a troll). Dress one child to look like the creature. Use an existing costume or create your own with color-coordinated clothes and construction paper for a hat or wings.

Take your two kids to a wide-open space with no one else around. You don't want someone wandering into the picture (or laughing at your crudely made construction-paper troll cap). Place your human kid near the camera with her hand flat out to the side as if she were holding something. Send your costumed kid into the distant background until she looks very small, then move her left or right until she appears to be standing in the human child's extended palm.

Have your subjects adjust their heads so they seem to be making eye contact and adjust their emotions so you can tell how they feel. Take a few photos, then let the kids trade roles. As you wait for the photo to be developed, make up a cool story about how the creature was discovered and why it was set free.

Lake Monster

WHAT YOU'LL NEED: A sock • Art supplies (markers, buttons, paint, sewing materials) • Camera

If you have an odd sock around the house (and who doesn't?), try your hand at recreating the famous photo of the Loch Ness Monster.

Decorate the sock to look like the head and neck of a dinosaur-like beast. Use art supplies to add eyes, teeth, fins, or scales. Dark, solid socks look most convincing, but a pink polka-dotted one can be just as fun.

Decide who will wear the sock (you or your child), then go jump in a lake (or a creek, or a pool). As the photographer holds the camera, the sock wearer holds his breath, submerges, and puts the creature into place by sticking a hand out of the water.

To keep the size and location a mystery, the photographer tries to take pictures that feature the creature and the water only. An inquisitive duck or distant diving board are likely to spoil the illusion. Snap pictures of the creature bursting to the surface, looking around, and diving below. Whether lurking in a lake or playing in a pool, your monster photo is sure to make a splash!

DUH (Dad's Useful Hints): Decide who does what job based on swimming skills and not photography skills. It is better to have a bad photo of a good swimmer wearing a sock, than a good picture of a sinking kid or dad!

Flying Saucer

WHAT YOU'LL NEED: A saucer-shaped object (a hat, trash lid, dog dish) • Art supplies (paint, glitter, buttons—metallic colors preferred)

Find something that looks like a saucer, then decorate it to disguise it from easy detection. Add paint, glitter, buttons, or anything to give it a metallic or machinelike look. Tie some fishing line to your saucer and hang it from a tree branch. Stand back so the string is not visible and snap the picture. The saucer will appear to be flying in the distance behind the tree.

For an action shot, have your child throw the saucer in the air so you can snap a photo when it comes into frame. If the final photo appears a bit blurry, tell everyone it was moving at a super speed.

DUH (Dad's Useful Hints): Do not use dishware to make your saucer. If Mom recognizes a place setting in your picture (whether you broke it or not), your camera will be abducted.

43
Strange and Silly Superstitions

The Lowdown on Lovable and Laughable Legends

Superstitions are irrationally nutty notions based on magic and chance. They are false conceptions of cause and effect that have survived for centuries without any basis in reality. They are also a lot of fun. Help your kids gather good fortune, avoid bad luck, and predict their future by turning these old wives' tales into Amazing Dad anecdotes.

Seven Things That Give Good Luck

(Teach the Kids and Try Them Out)

1. Eating black-eyed peas on New Year's Day.

2. Saying "Rabbit, rabbit," as your first words each month.

3. Throwing spilled salt over your left shoulder.

4. Lifting your feet and holding your breath while driving over a bridge. **DUH (Dad's Useful Hints):** It says "driving," not "diving."

5. Lifting your feet when a car you're in goes over a railroad track.

6. Finding a four-leaf clover.

7. The number seven.

Thirteen Things That Bring Bad Luck

(Warn the Kids and Be Wary)

1. Walking under a ladder.

2. Rocking a rocking chair with no one in it.

3. Crossing the path of a black cat. (Worse, if you are a mouse.)

4. Opening an umbrella in the house.

5. Leaving shoes on the table.

6. Putting a hat on a bed.

7. Breaking a mirror. (Seven years bad luck!)

8. Ignoring a chain letter. (Or its technologically advanced doppelganger, the dreaded chain E-mail!)

9. Spilling salt.

10. Hurting a ladybug.

11. Finding a bird flying in your house.

12. Waking up on the wrong side of the bed. (We're guessing the left side is the wrong side since it isn't right.)

13. The number thirteen.

Seven More Things That Give Good Luck

(So the Good Ones Outweigh the Bad!)

1. Finding a penny that is heads-up. (If it's tails, turn it over, and let your kid pick it up.)

2. Hanging a horseshoe over a door (like a *U* to hold luck in).

3. Seeing an elephant (real or fake) with its trunk up.

4. Noticing three butterflies together.

5. Carrying a rabbit's foot. (Not lucky for rabbits.)

6. Catching a cricket in your house.

7. Finding a frog in your house. (No word on what happens if the frog catches the cricket. We're guessing everyone gets a good night's sleep!)

A Dozen Omens

(Sure Signs Of Things To Come)

1. If your foot itches, you are going to take a trip.

2. If the palm of your hand itches, you will receive money.

3. If the back of your hand itches, you will lose money.

4. If your nose itches, someone is thinking about you.

5. If your left ear rings, someone is saying good things about you.

6. If your right ear rings, someone is saying bad things about you.

7. If you drop a spoon, a female will visit you.

8. If you drop a fork, a male will visit you.

9. If you drop a knife, you will break the spell (or cut your foot).

10. If you step over somebody, they won't grow.

11. If you step on a crack, you'll break your mother's back.

12. If you make that face, it will get stuck that way.

AMAZING DAD MOMENT
Keeping Me Safe

My father had three superstitions he said would keep me safe. Whenever we shared good news, he knocked on wood so spirits wouldn't hear us and try to spoil things.

If we walked hand in hand and something came between us, he'd say, "bread and butter," to keep his connection with me until our hands met again.

Whenever I left the house, he'd turn away before I was out of sight to ensure I returned safely.

I never believed these things really worked, but they showed that he loved me and would do anything to protect me, and that made me feel as safe as could be. Looking back, I believe that was his goal all along.

44
Go Wish

Wishing Well

Kids are rarely at a loss when it comes to thinking of things to wish for. The Amazing Dad has a special knack for finding things to wish *upon*.

Reasons to Wish

Here are a dozen reasons to make wishes, ranging from the obvious to the obscure.

Encourage your child to make a wish when he or she . . .

1. Blows out the candles on a birthday cake.

2. Blows on a dandelion.

3. Blows a fallen eyelash off a fingertip.

4. Sees a falling star.

5. Sees the first star of the evening.

6. Sees the first snowflake of winter.

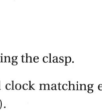

7. Sees the charm of a chain touching the clasp.

8. Sees the numbers on a digital clock matching each other (3:33, 5:55, special bonus wishing time, 11:11).

9. Tosses a penny in a fountain or wishing well.

10. Gets the larger half of a wishbone.

11. Catches a leprechaun.

12. Rubs a lamp and frees a genie.

The last two are a little rare. So we'll add one more and make it a baker's dozen. Speaking of baking, this one's as easy as pie: Next time your child gets a piece of pie, have him cut off the tip of the slice and set it aside. Explain that eating the "first bite" last, he will cause a shift in the time-space continuum creating a magical vortex that will allow him to make a single wish.

AMAZING DAD MOMENT
Magic Mail

My daughter makes a wish every time we get a letter with a stamp featuring a flower. I keep a stash of flower stamps hidden in my office and sneak them over existing stamps whenever I want to surprise her. It costs me thirty-four cents, but she's worth it! Family friends are aware of our ritual and use flower stamps whenever they write.

Creating Your Own Charms

A little ingenuity and imagination can convert ordinary objects or common occurrences into pure magic.

Find funny things that happen infrequently, wacky ones that happen weekly, or dependable ones that happen daily. Anoint these moments with magical powers, share them secretly with your son or daughter, and wish whenever you want.

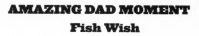

AMAZING DAD MOMENT
Fish Wish

The fish in our lake have magical powers. Whenever my son and I see one make a splash, we shout, "Fish Wish" and begin reciting the alphabet. I say, *A*, he says, *B*, and so on. If a fish splashes while someone is speaking, that person can wish for anything beginning with that letter.

The Rules of Wishing
(And How to Handle Them)

Somewhere in the realm of wishers past, a wise man put forth a proclamation stating that wishes should be made in silence. The wise man said that if we reveal what we wish for, the wish won't come true. Perhaps "wise man" is too kind a term.

While the wishes-should-remain-a-secret rule adds mystery to the process, it adds misery, too. It produces a plethora of perplexing problems. How do you grant wishes when you don't know what they are? Will you be able to grant them if you do find out? Should you try to grant them at all?

Here are three ideas for dealing with these dilemmas:

• **Hunt for Hints:** Converse casually about wishes prior to events so you have some idea what's on your child's mind.

• **Make up Rules:** "If we hold hands and wish at the same time, we're allowed to tell each other what we wished for."

• **Create Your Quotas:** Grant only the wishes which seem unselfish, grant one wish a month, or grant them according to your child's behavior.

You are the wizard in your own world of wishes:
Use your wisdom however you wish!

PART X

The Amazing Dad as

The Ultimate Friend

45
Just Between Us
A Clandestine Course in Covert Correspondence

Secret messages are a great way to bond with your child. They
let you share something that no one else knows; they allow
you to communicate when you are apart; and they add intrigue
and excitement to everyday routines. Take note of these ideas,
then pass them along to your kid.

Simple Ciphers

Ciphers are secret messages in which letters are replaced or
rearranged. Here are five of our favorites.

ABC 123

Replace each letter with a corresponding number. (Dad
becomes 414.)

A	B	C	D	E	F	G	H	I	J	K	L	M	N	O	P	Q	R	S	T	U	V	W	X	Y	Z
1	2	3	4	5	6	7	8	9	10	11	12	13	14	15	16	17	18	19	20	21	22	23	24	25	26

Looney Letter Swap

Replace each letter with a random new letter. Make a sheet that reveals the
code and send it ahead of the note.

A	B	C	D	E	F	G	H	I	J	K	L	M	N	O	P	Q	R	S	T	U	V	W	X	Y	Z
W	A	Q	X	Z	V	Y	P	R	L	N	J	K	M	I	O	T	H	G	U	F	E	D	C	S	B

Picture Switcher

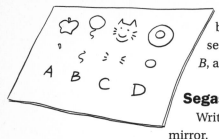

Think of a small picture beginning with each letter (an apple, a balloon, a cat, a doughnut). Use a portion of each picture to represent each letter (an apple stem = *A*, a balloon string = *B*, a cat's whiskers = *C*, a doughnut hole = *D*).

Segassem Sdrawkcab

Write backward so the message must be held up to a mirror.

Space Case

Write the sentence correctly but place spaces so that it looks like all the words have the same amount of letters. Add an *X* or two if you need it at the end. Tell your kid they're extra kisses!

IJU   STW   ROT   ETH   IST   OTE   LLY   OUI   LOV   EYO   UXX

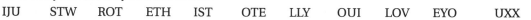

✳ POP TEN LIST
Ten Places to Put Secret Messages So Your Child Will Discover Them

1. In a lunch box.

2. In an E-mail or postcard.

3. In a favorite book.

4. In a cookie jar or cereal box.

5. In a shoe or clothes pocket.

6. In a CD or cassette case.

7. In a bottle floating in your pool.

8. Under a pillow.

9. Taped to a favorite toy.

10. Written in dust on a dresser.

Magical Messages

Invisible Ink
WHAT YOU'LL NEED: Toothpick • Lemon juice • White paper • Heat source (to reveal the message)

Dip the tip of a toothpick into lemon juice and write on a sheet of paper. The message will remain hidden until the paper is heated over a lamp.

DUH (Dad's Useful Hint): Assist in holding the paper over the lamp so your child doesn't burn his fingers, the paper, or the house.

Foggy Thought
WHAT YOU'LL NEED: Bar of soap • Bathroom mirror

Dampen the corner of a bar of soap, then lightly write on the bathroom mirror. As steam fills the bathroom during your child's hot bath, your message will magically appear in the glass.

Secret Signals

The Secret Knock
Create a crazy combination of knocks and responses so you will always know who is behind closed doors.

The Secret Password
Select an unusual word or phrase that must be uttered over the phone as a fun way to "verify" the voice on the other end of the line.

AMAZING DAD MOMENT
The Secret Handshake

When I was a kid, my father and I created a secret handshake. We shared it for years before I phased it out and forgot about it during my rebellious early teens.

Two decades later, I was visiting my parents' house when my six-year-old son said he wanted to show me something he had just learned from Grandpa. As my son gripped my hand, I knew exactly what it was.

The multistep moves came back in an instant and brought with them some of the most wonderful memories of my childhood. I found my father in the next room and thanked him by sharing the handshake for the first time in almost twenty years.

The three of us now share it regularly.

46

A Really Big Deal

Dad's Decoder Deck

Send a special message by creating a secret code with an ordinary deck of cards. Present the cards to your child, then help decipher the words that have been lost in the shuffle.

Create Your Decoder Deck

WHAT YOU'LL NEED: A deck of cards • A piece of paper • A thin marker • Rubber bands

Shuffle a full deck of cards. It doesn't have to be a full deck. This is the perfect opportunity to use that pack that's missing a few cards!

Write down the order of the cards from top to bottom.

Draw suits or write initials to make your list quick and easy to read.

Write Your Special Message

Wrap a couple of rubber bands, lengthwise, around the cards to hold them tightly in place. Use a thin marker to write on the sides of the deck.

For a longer message, cut the deck into separate piles, wrap them with rubber bands, and write a portion of the message on each stack.

Hide Your Message

Shuffle the cards so the words become a pattern of random lines. The message can only be read by returning the cards to the order you have written down.

Deliver the Deck

The Direct Method

Give your child a card box containing the scrambled deck along with the code-breaking card order so she can rearrange it right away.

The "Discovery" Method

Give your child a single card with instructions for finding the next card written across the face. Each card found will have directions for locating the next. (Look in the cookie jar; Check under your pillow; Go to the dictionary and look up the word *card*.) The final card discovered will lead your child to the location of the code.

Decode the Message

Help your child crack the code by stacking a couple of cards. Find the first card on the list and place it faceup. Find the second card on the list and place it faceup on the first. Follow suit until your child has caught on, then hand over the cards so your child can continue stacking.

Sit back and watch your child smile with wonder as your words magically appear. When the message is deciphered, put the cards in a special place, then work together to create a decoder deck with a special message for Mom.

1. I love you.

2. Happy birthday.

3. You make me proud.

4. We're going on vacation.

5. Grandma is coming to visit.

6. Your new bike is in the garage.

7. We're increasing your allowance.

8. You're going to have a baby sister.

9. Congratulations! You made the team.

10. Stop playing with cards and do your homework.

47

I Love You

Wonderful Ways to Share the Words

The Amazing Dad isn't ashamed to express his feelings to his kids. He's just ashamed to express them in a routine way. Whether you share the words in a silly, secret, or stylish manner, the message is always special. Here are some great ways to say I love you.

Write It Out

Put the words on sheets of paper. Hand them over openly, pass them out secretly, hang them up proudly, or hide them to be discovered unexpectedly.

Point It Out

Point to your eye. Point to your heart. Point to your child.

Hand It Out

Hold your fist up with your fingers folded toward your child. Raise the index finger to represent the letter *I.* Flip out the thumb to convert it to an *L* (for love.) Turn the hand so the tip of the index finger points directly to your child indicating *you*.

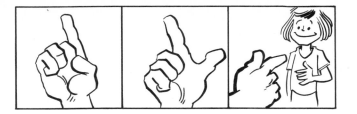

Count It Out

Show the numbers 1 4 3, held up on your fingers, displayed on a calculator, or sent via a beeper. The numbers coincide with the amount of letters in each of the words: I = 1, love = 4, you = 3.

Tap It Out

Use a phone or buzzer to send the message via Morse code.

```
 ..    .-..   ---    ....   .     .---   ---    ..-
 I      L      O      V     E      Y      O      U
```

Draw It Out

Draw an eye. Draw a heart. Draw a ewe. If your sheep doesn't look like a female, add long eyelashes and lipstick-heavy lips. If your sheep doesn't look like a sheep, draw a giant letter *U* instead.

Squeeze It Out

Squeeze your child's hand three times (one squeeze for each word). Slip squeezes in when you're walking hand in hand, circling up for games, or when saying grace. Your child can return the thought with four squeezes. (I love you, too!)

Sign It Out

Sound It Out

Share the three words with any noise in a series of three. (Three honks of the horn as you drive away, three pounds of the glove as you play catch, three taps of the spoon as you stir your morning coffee.)

Figure It Out

Substitute the words with an agreed-upon alternate phrase. ("My feet are itchy." "Got any gum?" "Somebody stepped on a pretzel.") Say the phrase in any situation and the two of you will be the only ones who know what it means.

Get It Out

The words are in your heart. Get them out so your child gets the message. Use the ideas listed above, or go with the strongest method of all: look in your child's eyes and simply say, "I love you."

1. **African**—Ek het jou lief.

2. **French**—Je t'adore.

3. **German**—Ich liebe dich.

4. **Hawaiian**—Aloha wau ia oi.

5. **Italian**—Ti amo.

6. **Japanese**—Aishiteru.

7. **Pig Latin**—Iay ovlay ouyay.

8. **Polish**—Kocham Ciebie.

9. **Russian**—Ya tebya liubliu.

10. **Spanish**—Te amo.

48

Not the Same Old Story

Truly Original, Original Tales

There are as many good times to tell a tale as there are good tales to tell. Share stories before bed, during trips, around campfires, at parties, on rainy days, and any other time that inspiration strikes. Here are some hints on spinning yarns that are uncommonly special.

Cliff-hangers

What's the best way for a storyteller to keep kids in suspense? We'll tell you later.

Ad-lib Story

Create original tales by stopping mid-sentence so your kid can fill in the blanks.

Example

Dad	Kid
Once upon a time there was a . . .	*Frog!*
The frog's name was . . .	*Hanna Banna!*
One day, Hanna Banna saw a . . .	*Giant pig riding a Swan!*

With a little practice, the tales and the teamwork will improve. She'll begin to anticipate the stops, and you'll see patterns in her thought process and alter plots accordingly. You'll never know exactly what to expect with an ad-lib story, but you can usually expect something wonderful.

Ad-lib Rhyme

This is easier than it sounds. Just start an original poem and lead your kid in the right direction so he can supply the rhyming word to end each sentence.

Example

Dad	Kid
Once there was a silly . . .	*Cat!*
On his head he wore a . . .	*Hat!*
The color of the hat was . . .	*White!*
It hurt because it was too . . .	*Tight!*

If your child suggests difficult words like *orange* or *elephant,* encourage him to create nonsense words to complete the rhymes. (Dr. Seuss does it!) A ladybug from planet Shadyhug is brilliantly silly enough to make an improbably remarkable poem.

Makeup Mix-up

Make a big deal about telling an *original* story, then "accidentally" slip in details from famous movies or books. Keep up the silly give-and-take until you've "borrowed" enough ideas to create a truly original story.

Dad	**Kid**
I made up the best story!	*Just go Dad.*
Once there was a girl named Rapunzel.	*I heard this one.*
She lived in a house with seven dwarves.	*That's Snow White!*
The house got blown away by a big bad wolf . . .	*Three pigs! Three pigs!*
Then landed on a wicked witch in Munchkinland!	*Wizard of Oz!*

True-life Family Adventures

MOM SWEPT ME OFF MY FEET...

Share stories that have happened to people you know. You don't have to make them up. You just have to remember them.

Begin by telling your child about things that happened when she was younger (her first day of school, her second birthday, the home run she hit last week). She'll be happy to fill in forgotten details and correct those you get wrong.

You can toss in tales from your childhood, recap romantic misadventures with Mom, and tell classic tales of close relatives. No matter who the hero of a true-life adventure may be, the stories will preserve your family history for future generations to enjoy.

Cliff-hangers, Continued

Create a cliff-hanger to capture your kid's attention and keep him wondering what will happen next. Find a colorful continuing character (a superhero, a scientist, your child in the starring role). Send the character on an adventure, build the action to a peak, then stop.

Toss out a rhetorical question or two ("Has our hero finally met her match?" "Will the plot to pilfer the giant pickle actually succeed?"), then end with a "Tune in tomorrow to find out!"

The time between tales gives your child a chance to imagine (or dream) about the adventure and gives you a chance to plan how you'll get the hero out of the mess you've created. Try beginning new adventures every Monday night, concluding them on Friday, and taking weekends off to work up ideas for the next go around.

49

Off the Wall

Brighten the Night with Shadows

The night may be dark, but there is no need for it to be gloomy. A little imagination can always lighten things up. Use a flashlight, a night-light, or some lamplight to create shadows that are sure to cast a spell.

The Incredible Growing Child

Point a light at your child's back to project a life-sized shadow on the wall. Move toward her, bringing your hand down, but angling the light up. Her shadow will appear to grow. By the time you reach the ground near her feet, her head will be towering on the ceiling above you.

The Amazing Morphing Man

Stand your child in front of a light so he is looking at his shadow. Stand directly behind him so your shadow covers his completely. Lean your bodies and extend your extremities to create The Man with Four Legs, The Man with Three Arms, or The Man with Two Heads.

The Wonderfully Hungry Head

Sit in front of a light so your child sees a large profile of your head on the wall. Hold up an object so its shadow is clearly visible in your fingers, then bring it toward your wide-open mouth.

Let the object vanish into the shadow of your head so it appears that you have swallowed it. Complete the illusion by revealing your empty hands, smacking your lips, or letting out a belch.

Start small by gulping down an action figure or a wooden block, slowly increasing the size of your snacks until you are swallowing toy trucks, beach balls, and stuffed animals.

Hand Shadows

Try a few of these handy hints for creating creatures of the night.

Wildcat

Alligator

Hare

Tortoise

Bird

Paper Shadows

WHAT YOU'LL NEED: Study paper • Popsicle sticks • Glue or tape • Scissors

Shadow puppets are a great way to share a story. We've created a few classic characters so you can concentrate on creating a classic tale. Photocopy and enlarge the pictures on sturdy paper, cut them out, and attach them to Popsicle sticks. Cast their shadows on the wall and begin your adventure.

Boy

Girl

Dog

Cat

Mouse

Horse

Dragon

50

The Amazing Dad's Grand Finale

Great Ways to End the Days

There is a "good night" at the end of every great day. The time spent getting your child to wind down doesn't have to wind up being dull. Here are some suggestions to make the final moments of the day some of the most memorable.

Seven Surprises for Seven Nights

Create a little excitement with a new activity every night. Sit with your child each Sunday and think of seven things the two of you could do together to make an evening special. Write each idea on a scrap of paper, fold them up, and place them in a hat. (Call it a nightcap!)

Have your child draw one suggestion from the hat each evening. Whatever is selected should be thoroughly completed and thoroughly enjoyed before bedtime. Refill the hat every Sunday, adding new ideas or reentering suggestions that were especially fun.

Here are seven ideas to get you started:

1. Read an extra book.

2. Play a favorite game.

3. Dance to a selected song.

4. Search for bugs with a flashlight.

5. Look for constellations or falling stars.

6. Take a backyard, midnight piggyback ride.

7. Stay up fifteen minutes late.

AMAZING DAD MOMENT
Rock-'n'-Roll Lullaby

When I was a little girl, my parents used to take turns singing me to sleep. Though Mom stuck to traditional lullabies, Dad's repertoire consisted mostly of rock songs sung in a soft whisper.

Mom used to joke about Dad's song choices, but I believe he just wanted to introduce me to the music he loved. The songs always seemed like kid songs to me, anyway. By the time I was four, I knew lyrics to "Yellow Submarine," "Magic Bus," "Bridge Over Troubled Water," and countless others.

If we were driving in the car and a disc jockey played one of the records, Dad and I would make a big deal of singing along together.

Today, I sing rock lullabies to my own kids, and am flooded with fond memories whenever I hear one of Dad's "good-night songs" on the radio.

POP TEN LIST
Ten Classic Good-Night Kisses

1. **Fish Kiss**—Playfully peck at him with thin puckered lips.

2. **Butterfly Kiss**—Tickle her tenderly with blinking eyelashes.

3. **Eskimo Kiss**—Gently rub your nose against his.

4. **Blow a Kiss**—Stand at a distance, place a kiss on your fingertips, and blow it in her direction.

5. Throw a Kiss—Stand at a distance, place a kiss on your fingertips, wind up, and hurl it his way.

6. Kiss Monster—Make strange noises and silly faces as you place fast and funny kisses all over her face.

7. Raspberry Surprise—Lean in to kiss his cheek but plant a rousing raspberry instead.

8. Miss Kiss—Try to kiss her forehead but kiss her hair. Try to kiss her cheek but kiss her ear. Try to kiss her lips but kiss her nose.

9. Motor Kiss—Tug your ear and start your lips like a motor. Flap them noisily until they've made contact with his cheek.

10. Bait and Switch—Ask her for a kiss on the cheek. Turn your head at the last moment so it lands on your lips.

The Amazing Dad's Good-Night Poem

As the moon becomes bright,
My arms won't let go.
They cling to the day that we had.
As I tuck you in tight,
My smile lets you know
How great it is being your dad.
As I turn off the light,
My mind's thinking of
All the wonderful things that we did.
As I kiss you good night,
My heart's full of love,
All for you, my Amazing Kid.

Conclusion

If you are reading this page, you have either

A. Finished the book.

B. Skipped over a bunch of chapters.

C. Started reading from the wrong end.

If none of these answers apply to you, then we've jumped to the wrong conclusion. Hopefully, you've jumped to the right one. So read on!

Passing It On

You are The Amazing Dad! You have mastered the secrets! You've shared the moments! You have created the memories! What do you do now? You pass them on!

As The Amazing Dad, you cannot keep your secrets forever. Believe it or not, there will be a day when you will want to come clean to your kids about the source of your superpowers. You'll put it off for as long as you can. You'll convince yourself that the right moment just hasn't arrived. But someday, when your kids have kids of their own, you'll realize that it is the right thing to do.

Teaching grown children the secrets behind tricks that have baffled them for years is one of life's little pleasures. It is usually followed by an even sweeter reward; watching your children perform the same feats for *their* kids.

Protect your Amazing Dad secrets when your child needs you to be a hero. Pass the secrets on when your child is ready to become one. When the time comes, take this book from its hiding spot and give it to your child.

If your kid seems surprised to discover that many of your best bits came from a book, simply claim that you're an old friend of ours and that we based a majority of the stuff on you anyway!

It's now in your child's hands. Have faith. Your kid will continue your work.

The moments you have shared are etched in your child's mind. The love you have shown is planted in your child's heart. You've left a legacy of wonder and laughter that will remain with your family forever.

Kick back and bask in the glory. You are truly The Amazing Dad.

Special Thanks

We would like to give special thanks to the following people for their ideas, comments, suggestions, stories, grammar corrections, encouragement, patience, advice, love, and inspiration. For without them, this book would not have been possible. THANK YOU! XOXOXO

Sherrell Preuss	Orvel Ray Wilson	Danny Archer	Aye Jaye
Jaret Preuss	Eric Mead	David Williamson	Johnny "Ace" Palmer
Tracy Livera	Doc Eason	Terry Ward	The team at Perigee Books
Carol Livera	Harrison Carroll	John Ekin	
Michelle Livera	Tim Conover	All of our friends at SCT	Pat Williams
Michael Livera	Eugene Burger		Hayley Fensch
Bobby Livera	Martin Gardner	Scott Sugiuchi	Kris French
Petra Livera	Pat Williams	Rob Smith Jr.	Jamie Fensch
Cris Shank	Toni Crippen	Rob's girlfriend	Judy Frank
Alan James Novotny	Toni Brent	Jay Marshall	Christopher Murphy
Harold Wilhelm	Tim Hill	Todd Baker	Beth Vaughn
Allison Auld	Kerry Pollock	Greg Godek	Wendy Gray
Terri Risius	Randy Schwagger	Mike Larsen	Janine Brown
Mark S.A. Smith	Dave Davidson	Elizabeth Pomada	Pat Franklin

The Students at Discovery Middle School

Be in Our Next Book!

Thank you for purchasing *The Amazing Dad*. We hope you enjoyed reading it as much as we enjoyed writing it. If you received this book as a gift, please give your gift giver a hug for us. If you acquired it by shoplifting, you have made a poor career choice, but an excellent literary selection.

We hope *The Amazing Dad* will bring you and your family joyous moments for years to come. We are already hard at play on its sequel. We are discovering secrets, inventing tricks, and collecting *Amazing Dad Moments* from fathers just like you.

If reading our book brought back fond memories of *Amazing Dad Moments* in your own life, we'd love to put it in our next book. Send us a moment that you've shared with your children and inspire fathers throughout the world. Send in a moment you've remembered from your childhood and it will stand as a tribute to your own Amazing Dad.

If you have a memory to share, a question to ask, or a few minutes to surf the net before the boss comes by, please visit our web site at ***www.amazingdad.com.***

If your ideas are used in the sequel, you will receive our heartfelt thanks, a published credit, and, best yet, ***a free copy of the book!!!***

Index

Page numbers in *italic* indicate illustrations.

Giovanni Livera is a world champion magician and corporate entertainer. His motivational program "Be Amazing" teaches audiences that "anything is possible." A member of the National Speakers Association, Giovanni gives 150 speeches annually, and his clients include American Express, Dell Computer, Pepsi-Cola, and Walt Disney Corporation. Visit his web site at www.wowmom.com.

Ken Preuss is a middle school teacher and professional children's performer. He has published several plays for children, and helped create "Reading, It's Magic," an educational and entertaining program that he took to elementary schools and libraries throughout Florida. Ken lives in Florida with his wife, Sherrell, and spends his free time being an Amazing Dad to his son, Jaret.